CHARITY IN TRUTH

Caritas in Veritate

ENCYCLICAL LETTER

CHARITY IN TRUTH

Caritas in Veritate

OF THE SUPREME PONTIFF
BENEDICT XVI
TO THE BISHOPS
PRIESTS AND DEACONS
MEN AND WOMEN RELIGIOUS
THE LAY FAITHFUL
AND ALL PEOPLE OF GOOD WILL
ON INTEGRAL HUMAN DEVELOPMENT
IN CHARITY AND TRUTH

LIBRERIA EDITRICE VATICANA
IGNATIUS PRESS   SAN FRANCISCO

Front cover art: Papal Coat of Arms of Pope Benedict XVI
by AgnusImages.com

Back cover photograph: Photograph of Pope Benedict XVI
by Stefano Spaziani

Cover design by Roxanne Mei Lum

Published in 2009 by Ignatius Press, San Francisco
© 2009 by Libreria Editrice Vaticana, Vatican City
ISBN 978-1-58617-280-0
Library of Congress Control Number 2008926716
Printed in the United States of America ∞

CONTENTS

INTRODUCTION

1. Charity in truth, to which Jesus Christ bore witness by his earthly life and especially by his death and resurrection, is the principal driving force behind the authentic development of every person and of all humanity. Love—*caritas*—is an extraordinary force which leads people to opt for courageous and generous engagement in the field of justice and peace. It is a force that has its origin in God, Eternal Love and Absolute Truth. Each person finds his good by adherence to God's plan for him, in order to realize it fully: in this plan, he finds his truth, and through adherence to this truth he becomes free (cf. *Jn* 8:22). To defend the truth, to articulate it with humility and conviction, and to bear witness to it in life are therefore exacting and indispensable forms of charity. Charity, in fact, "rejoices in the truth" (*1 Cor* 13:6). All people feel the interior impulse to love authentically: love and truth never abandon them completely, because these are the vocation planted by God in the heart and mind of every human person. The search for love and truth is purified and liberated by Jesus Christ from the impoverishment that our humanity brings to it, and he reveals to us in all its fullness the initiative of love

and the plan for true life that God has prepared for us. In Christ, *charity in truth* becomes the Face of his Person, a vocation for us to love our brothers and sisters in the truth of his plan. Indeed, he himself is the Truth (cf. *Jn* 14:6).

2. Charity is at the heart of the Church's social doctrine. Every responsibility and every commitment spelled out by that doctrine is derived from charity, which, according to the teaching of Jesus, is the synthesis of the entire Law (cf. *Mt* 22:36–40). It gives real substance to the personal relationship with God and with neighbor; it is the principle not only of micro-relationships (with friends, with family members, or within small groups), but also of macro-relationships (social, economic, and political ones). For the Church, instructed by the Gospel, charity is everything because, as Saint John teaches (cf. *1 Jn* 4:8, 16) and as I recalled in my first Encyclical Letter, *God Is Love* (*Deus Caritas Est*): *everything has its origin in God's love, everything is shaped by it, everything is directed towards it.* Love is God's greatest gift to humanity, it is his promise and our hope.

I am aware of the ways in which charity has been and continues to be misconstrued and emptied of meaning, with the consequent risk of being misinterpreted, detached from ethical living, and, in any event, undervalued. In the social, juridical, cultural, political, and economic fields— the contexts, in other words, that are most exposed to this danger—it is easily dismissed as irrelevant for interpreting and giving direction to moral responsibility. Hence the need to link charity with truth not only in the sequence, pointed out by Saint Paul, of *veritas in caritate* (*Eph* 4:15), but also in the inverse and complementary sequence of *caritas in veritate*. Truth needs to be sought, found, and expressed within the "economy" of charity, but charity in its turn needs to be understood, confirmed, and practiced in the light of truth. In this way, not only do we do a service to charity enlightened by truth, but also we help give credibility to truth, demonstrating its persuasive and authenticating power in the practical setting of social living. This is a matter of no small account today, in a social and cultural context which relativizes truth, often paying little heed to it and showing increasing reluctance to acknowledge its existence.

3. Through this close link with truth, charity can be recognized as an authentic expression of humanity and as an element of fundamental importance in human relations, including those of a public nature. *Only in truth does charity shine*

forth, only in truth can charity be authentically lived. Truth is the light that gives meaning and value to charity. That light is both the light of reason and the light of faith, through which the intellect attains to the natural and supernatural truth of charity: it grasps its meaning as gift, acceptance, and communion. Without truth, charity degenerates into sentimentality. Love becomes an empty shell, to be filled in an arbitrary way. In a culture without truth, this is the fatal risk facing love. It falls prey to contingent subjective emotions and opinions; the word "love" is abused and distorted, to the point where it comes to mean the opposite. Truth frees charity from the constraints of an emotionalism that deprives it of relational and social content and of a fideism that deprives it of human and universal breathing-space. In the truth, charity reflects the personal yet public dimension of faith in the God of the Bible, who is both *Agápe* and *Lógos*: Charity and Truth, Love and Word.

4. Because it is filled with truth, charity can be understood in the abundance of its values, it can be shared and communicated. *Truth*, in fact, is *lógos*, which creates *diá-logos* and, hence, communication and communion. Truth, by enabling men and women to let go of their subjective opinions and impressions, allows them

to move beyond cultural and historical limitations and to come together in the assessment of the value and substance of things. Truth opens and unites our minds in the *lógos* of love: this is the Christian proclamation and testimony of charity. In the present social and cultural context, where there is a widespread tendency to relativize truth, practicing charity in truth helps people to understand that adhering to the values of Christianity is not merely useful but essential for building a good society and for true integral human development. A Christianity of charity without truth would be more or less interchangeable with a pool of good sentiments, helpful for social cohesion, but of little relevance. In other words, there would no longer be any real place for God in the world. Without truth, charity is confined to a narrow field devoid of relations. It is excluded from the plans and processes of promoting human development of universal range, in dialogue between knowledge and praxis.

5. Charity is love received and given. It is "grace" (*cháris*). Its source is the wellspring of the Father's love for the Son, in the Holy Spirit. Love comes down to us from the Son. It is creative love, through which we have our being; it is redemptive love, through which we are recreated. Love

is revealed and made present by Christ (cf. *Jn* 13:1) and "poured into our hearts through the Holy Spirit" (*Rom* 5:5). As the objects of God's love, men and women become subjects of charity; they are called to make themselves instruments of grace, so as to pour forth God's charity and to weave networks of charity.

This dynamic of charity received and given is what gives rise to the Church's social teaching, which is *caritas in veritate in re sociali*: the proclamation of the truth of Christ's love in society. This doctrine is a service to charity, but its locus is truth. Truth preserves and expresses charity's power to liberate in the ever-changing events of history. It is at the same time the truth of faith and of reason, both in the distinction and also in the convergence of those two cognitive fields. Development, social well-being, the search for a satisfactory solution to the grave socioeconomic problems besetting humanity, all need this truth. What they need even more is that this truth should be loved and demonstrated. Without truth, without trust and love for what is true, there is no social conscience and responsibility, and social action ends up serving private interests and the logic of power, resulting in social fragmentation, especially in a globalized society at difficult times like the present.

6. "*Caritas in veritate*" is the principle around which the Church's social doctrine turns, a principle that takes on practical form in the criteria that govern moral action. I would like to consider two of these in particular, of special relevance to the commitment to development in an increasingly globalized society: *justice and the common good.*

First of all, justice. *Ubi societas, ibi ius*: every society draws up its own system of justice. *Charity goes beyond justice*, because to love is to give, to offer what is "mine" to the other; but it never lacks justice, which prompts us to give the other what is "his", what is due to him by reason of his being or his acting. I cannot "give" what is mine to the other without first giving him what pertains to him in justice. If we love others with charity, then first of all we are just towards them. Not only is justice not extraneous to charity, not only is it not an alternative or parallel path to charity: justice is inseparable from charity[1] and intrinsic to it. Justice is the primary way of charity, or, in Paul VI's words, "the minimum

---

[1] Cf. Paul VI, Encyclical Letter *Populorum Progressio* (26 March 1967), 22: *AAS* 59 (1967), 268; Second Vatican Ecumenical Council, Pastoral Constitution on the Church in the Modern World *Gaudium et Spes*, 69.

measure" of it,[2] an integral part of the love "in deed and in truth" (*1 Jn* 3:18) to which Saint John exhorts us. On the one hand, charity demands justice: recognition and respect for the legitimate rights of individuals and peoples. It strives to build the *earthly city* according to law and justice. On the other hand, charity transcends justice and completes it in the logic of giving and forgiving.[3] The *earthly city* is promoted not merely by relationships of rights and duties, but to an even greater and more fundamental extent by relationships of gratuitousness, mercy, and communion. Charity always manifests God's love in human relationships as well; it gives theological and salvific value to all commitment for justice in the world.

7. Another important consideration is the common good. To love someone is to desire that person's good and to take effective steps to secure it. Besides the good of the individual, there is a good that is linked to living in society: the common good. It is the good of "all of us", made up of individuals, families, and intermediate

---

[2] *Address for the Day of Development* (23 August 1968): *AAS* 60 (1968), 626–627.

[3] Cf. John Paul II, *Message for the 2002 World Day of Peace: AAS* 94 (2002), 132–140.

groups who together constitute society.[4] It is a good that is sought, not for its own sake, but for the people who belong to the social community and who can only really and effectively pursue their good within it. To desire the *common good* and strive towards it *is a requirement of justice and charity*. To take a stand for the common good is, on the one hand, to be solicitous for and, on the other hand, to avail oneself of that complex of institutions that give structure to the life of society, juridically, civilly, politically, and culturally, making it the *pólis*, or "city". The more we strive to secure a common good corresponding to the real needs of our neighbors, the more effectively we love them. Every Christian is called to practice this charity, in a manner corresponding to his vocation and according to the degree of influence he wields in the *pólis*. This is the institutional path—we might also call it the political path—of charity, no less excellent and effective than the kind of charity which encounters the neighbor directly, outside the institutional mediation of the *pólis*. When animated by charity, commitment to the common good has greater worth than a merely secular and political stand would have. Like all commitment to

---

[4] Cf. Second Vatican Ecumenical Council, Pastoral Constitution on the Church in the Modern World *Gaudium et Spes*, 26.

justice, it has a place within the testimony of divine charity that paves the way for eternity through temporal action. Man's earthly activity, when inspired and sustained by charity, contributes to the building of the universal *city of God*, which is the goal of the history of the human family. In an increasingly globalized society, the common good and the effort to obtain it cannot fail to assume the dimensions of the whole human family, that is to say, the community of peoples and nations,[5] in such a way as to shape the *earthly city* in unity and peace, rendering it to some degree an anticipation and a prefiguration of the undivided *city of God*.

8. In 1967, when he issued the Encyclical *Populorum Progressio*, my venerable predecessor Pope Paul VI illuminated the great theme of the development of peoples with the splendor of truth and the gentle light of Christ's charity. He taught that life in Christ is the first and principal factor of development,[6] and he entrusted us with the task of travelling the path of development with all our heart and all our intelligence,[7] that is to say, with

---

[5] Cf. John XXIII, Encyclical Letter *Pacem in Terris* (11 April 1963): *AAS* 55 (1963), 268–270.

[6] Cf. no. 16: *loc. cit.*, 265.

[7] Cf. *ibid.*, 82: *loc. cit.*, 297.

the ardor of charity and the wisdom of truth. It is the primordial truth of God's love, grace bestowed upon us, that opens our lives to gift and makes it possible to hope for a "development of the whole man and of all men",[8] to hope for progress "from less human conditions to those which are more human",[9] obtained by overcoming the difficulties that are inevitably encountered along the way.

At a distance of over forty years from the Encyclical's publication, I intend to pay tribute to and to honor the memory of the great Pope Paul VI, revisiting his teachings on *integral human development* and taking my place within the path that they marked out, so as to apply them to the present moment. This continuing application to contemporary circumstances began with the Encyclical *Sollicitudo Rei Socialis*, with which the Servant of God Pope John Paul II chose to mark the twentieth anniversary of the publication of *Populorum Progressio*. Until that time, only *Rerum Novarum* had been commemorated in this way. Now that a further twenty years have passed, I express my conviction that *Populorum Progressio* deserves to be considered "the *Rerum Novarum*

---

[8] *Ibid.*, 42: *loc. cit.*, 278.
[9] *Ibid.*, 20: *loc. cit.*, 267.

of the present age", shedding light upon humanity's journey towards unity.

9. Love in truth—*caritas in veritate*—is a great challenge for the Church in a world that is becoming progressively and pervasively globalized. The risk for our time is that the *de facto* interdependence of people and nations is not matched by ethical interaction of consciences and minds that would give rise to truly human development. Only in *charity, illumined by the light of reason and faith*, is it possible to pursue development goals that possess a more humane and humanizing value. The sharing of goods and resources, from which authentic development proceeds, is guaranteed, not by merely technical progress and relationships of utility, but by the potential of love that overcomes evil with good (cf. *Rom* 12:21), opening up the path towards reciprocity of consciences and liberties.

The Church does not have technical solutions to offer[10] and does not claim "to interfere in

---

[10] Cf. Second Vatican Ecumenical Council, Pastoral Constitution on the Church in the Modern World *Gaudium et Spes*, 36; Paul VI, Apostolic Letter *Octogesima Adveniens* (14 May 1971), 4: *AAS* 63 (1971), 403–404; John Paul II, Encyclical Letter *Centesimus Annus* (1 May 1991), 43: *AAS* 83 (1991), 847.

any way in the politics of States".[11] She does, however, have a mission of truth to accomplish, in every time and circumstance, for a society that is attuned to man, to his dignity, to his vocation. Without truth, it is easy to fall into an empiricist and skeptical view of life, incapable of rising to the level of praxis because of a lack of interest in grasping the values— sometimes even the meanings—with which to judge and direct it. Fidelity to man requires *fidelity to the truth*, which alone is the *guarantee of freedom* (cf. *Jn* 8:32) and of *the possibility of integral human development*. For this reason the Church searches for truth, proclaims it tirelessly, and recognizes it wherever it is manifested. This mission of truth is something that the Church can never renounce. Her social doctrine is a particular dimension of this proclamation: it is a service to the truth which sets us free. Open to the truth, from whichever branch of knowledge it comes, the Church's social doctrine receives it, assembles into a unity the fragments in which it is often found, and mediates it within the constantly changing life-patterns of the society of peoples and nations.[12]

---

[11] Paul VI, Encyclical Letter *Populorum Progressio*, 13: *loc. cit.*, 263–264.

[12] Cf. Pontifical Council for Justice and Peace, *Compendium of the Social Doctrine of the Church*, 76.

CHAPTER ONE

The Message of *Populorum Progressio*

10. A fresh reading of *Populorum Progressio*, more than forty years after its publication, invites us to remain faithful to its message of charity and truth, viewed within the overall context of Paul VI's specific magisterium and, more generally, within the tradition of the Church's social doctrine. Moreover, an evaluation is needed of the different terms in which the problem of development is presented today, as compared with forty years ago. The correct viewpoint, then, is that of the *Tradition of the apostolic faith*,[13] a patrimony both ancient and new, outside of which *Populorum Progressio* would be a document without roots—and issues concerning development would be reduced to merely sociological data.

11. The publication of *Populorum Progressio* occurred immediately after the conclusion of the Second Vatican Ecumenical Council, and in its opening paragraphs it clearly indicates its close

---

[13] Cf. Benedict XVI, *Address at the Inauguration of the Fifth General Conference of the Bishops of Latin America and the Caribbean* (Aparecida, 13 May 2007).

connection with the Council.[14] Twenty years later, in *Sollicitudo Rei Socialis*, John Paul II, in his turn, emphasized the earlier Encyclical's fruitful relationship with the Council, and especially with the Pastoral Constitution *Gaudium et Spes*.[15] I too wish to recall here the importance of the Second Vatican Council for Paul VI's Encyclical and for the whole of the subsequent social Magisterium of the Popes. The Council probed more deeply what had always belonged to the truth of the faith, namely, that the Church, being at God's service, is at the service of the world in terms of love and truth. Paul VI set out from this vision in order to convey two important truths. The first is that *the whole Church, in all her being and acting—when she proclaims, when she celebrates, when she performs works of charity—is engaged in promoting integral human development.* She has a public role over and above her charitable and educational activities: all the energy she brings to the advancement of humanity and of universal fraternity is manifested when she is able to operate in a climate of freedom. In not a few cases, that freedom is impeded by prohibitions and persecutions, or it is limited when the

---

[14] Cf. nos. 3–5: *loc. cit.,* 258–260.

[15] Cf. John Paul II, Encyclical Letter *Sollicitudo Rei Socialis* (30 December 1987), 6–7: *AAS* 80 (1988), 517–519.

Church's public presence is reduced to her charitable activities alone. The second truth is that *authentic human development concerns the whole of the person in every single dimension.*[16] Without the perspective of eternal life, human progress in this world is denied breathing-space. Enclosed within history, it runs the risk of being reduced to the mere accumulation of wealth; humanity thus loses the courage to be at the service of higher goods, at the service of the great and disinterested initiatives called forth by universal charity. Man does not develop through his own powers, nor can development simply be handed to him. In the course of history, it was often maintained that the creation of institutions was sufficient to guarantee the fulfillment of humanity's right to development. Unfortunately, too much confidence was placed in those institutions, as if they were able to deliver the desired objective automatically. In reality, institutions by themselves are not enough, because integral human development is primarily a vocation, and therefore it involves a free assumption of responsibility in solidarity on the part of everyone. Moreover, such development requires a transcendent vision of the person; it needs God: without him, development is

---

[16] Cf. Paul VI, Encyclical Letter *Populorum Progressio*, 14: *loc. cit.*, 264.

either denied or entrusted exclusively to man, who falls into the trap of thinking he can bring about his own salvation and ends up promoting a dehumanized form of development. Only through an encounter with God are we able to see in the other something more than just another creature,[17] to recognize the divine image in the other, thus truly coming to discover him or her and to mature in a love that "becomes concern and care for the other".[18]

12. The link between *Populorum Progressio* and the Second Vatican Council does not mean that Paul VI's social magisterium marked a break with that of previous Popes, because the Council constitutes a deeper exploration of this magisterium within the continuity of the Church's life.[19] In this sense, clarity is not served by certain abstract subdivisions of the Church's social doctrine, which apply categories to Papal social teaching that are extraneous to it. It is not a case of two typologies of social doctrine, one pre-conciliar and one post-conciliar, differing from one another: on the contrary, there is *a single*

---

[17] Cf. Benedict XVI, Encyclical Letter *Deus Caritas Est* (25 December 2005), 18: *AAS* 98 (2006), 232.

[18] *Ibid.*, 6: *loc cit.*, 222.

[19] Cf. Benedict XVI, *Christmas Address to the Roman Curia*, 22 December 2005.

teaching, consistent and at the same time ever new.[20] It is one thing to draw attention to the particular characteristics of one Encyclical or another, of the teaching of one Pope or another, but quite another to lose sight of the coherence of the overall doctrinal *corpus.*[21] Coherence does not mean a closed system: on the contrary, it means dynamic faithfulness to a light received. The Church's social doctrine illuminates with an unchanging light the new problems that are constantly emerging.[22] This safeguards the permanent and historical character of the doctrinal "patrimony"[23] which, with its specific characteristics, is part and parcel of the Church's everliving Tradition.[24] Social doctrine is built on the foundation handed on by the Apostles to the Fathers of the Church and then received and further explored by the great Christian doctors. This doctrine points definitively to the New Man, to the "last Adam [who] became a life-giving spirit" (*1 Cor* 15:45), the principle of the charity that "never ends" (*1 Cor* 13:8). It is attested by the

---

[20] Cf. John Paul II, Encyclical Letter *Sollicitudo Rei Socialis*, 3: *loc. cit.*, 515.

[21] Cf. *ibid.*, 1: *loc. cit.*, 513–514.

[22] Cf. *ibid.*, 3: *loc. cit.*, 515.

[23] Cf. John Paul II, Encyclical Letter *Laborem Exercens* (14 September 1981), 3: *AAS* 73 (1981), 583–584.

[24] Cf. John Paul II, Encyclical Letter *Centesimus Annus*, 3: *loc. cit.*, 794–796.

saints and by those who gave their lives for Christ our Savior in the field of justice and peace. It is an expression of the prophetic task of the Supreme Pontiffs to give apostolic guidance to the Church of Christ and to discern the new demands of evangelization. For these reasons, *Populorum Progressio*, situated within the great current of Tradition, can still speak to us today.

13. In addition to its important link with the entirety of the Church's social doctrine, *Populorum Progressio* is *closely connected to the overall magisterium of Paul VI*, especially his social magisterium. His was certainly a social teaching of great importance: he underlined the indispensable importance of the Gospel for building a society according to freedom and justice, in the ideal and historical perspective of a civilization animated by love. Paul VI clearly understood that the social question had become worldwide,[25] and he grasped the interconnection between the impetus towards the unification of humanity and the Christian ideal of a single family of peoples in solidarity and fraternity. *In the notion of development, understood in human and Christian terms, he identified the heart of the Christian social message,* and he proposed Christian charity as the

---

[25] Cf. Encyclical Letter *Populorum Progressio*, 3: *loc. cit.*, 258.

principal force at the service of development. Motivated by the wish to make Christ's love fully visible to contemporary men and women, Paul VI addressed important ethical questions robustly, without yielding to the cultural weaknesses of his time.

14. In his Apostolic Letter *Octogesima Adveniens* of 1971, Paul VI reflected on the meaning of politics and the *danger constituted by utopian and ideological visions* that place its ethical and human dimensions in jeopardy. These are matters closely connected with development. Unfortunately the negative ideologies continue to flourish. Paul VI had already warned against the technocratic ideology so prevalent today,[26] fully aware of the great danger of entrusting the entire process of development to technology alone, because in that way it would lack direction. Technology, viewed in itself, is ambivalent. If, on the one hand, some today would be inclined to entrust the entire process of development to technology, on the other hand, we are witnessing an upsurge of ideologies that deny *in toto* the very value of development, viewing it as radically anti-human and merely a source of degradation. This leads to a rejection, not only of the distorted and unjust

---

[26] Cf. *ibid.*, 34: *loc. cit.*, 274.

way in which progress is sometimes directed, but
also of scientific discoveries themselves, which,
if well used, could serve as an opportunity of
growth for all. The idea of a world without
development indicates a lack of trust in man and
in God. It is therefore a serious mistake to under-
value the human capacity to exercise control over
the deviations of development or to overlook the
fact that man is constitutionally oriented towards
"being more". Idealizing technical progress or
contemplating the utopia of a return to humanity's original natural state are two contrasting ways
of detaching progress from its moral evaluation
and hence from our responsibility.

15. Two further documents by Paul VI without any direct link to social doctrine—the
Encyclical *Humanae Vitae* (25 July 1968) and
the Apostolic Exhortation *Evangelii Nuntiandi*
(8 December 1975)—are highly important for
delineating the *fully human meaning of the development that the Church proposes*. It is therefore
helpful to consider these texts too in relation
to *Populorum Progressio*.

The Encyclical *Humanae Vitae* emphasizes both
the unitive and the procreative meaning of sexuality, thereby locating at the foundation of
society the married couple, man and woman,

who accept one another mutually, in distinction and in complementarity: a couple, therefore, that is open to life.[27] This is not a question of purely individual morality: *Humanae Vitae* indicates the *strong links between life ethics and social ethics*, ushering in a new area of magisterial teaching that has gradually been articulated in a series of documents, most recently John Paul II's Encyclical *Evangelium Vitae*.[28] The Church forcefully maintains this link between life ethics and social ethics, fully aware that "a society lacks solid foundations when, on the one hand, it asserts values such as the dignity of the person, justice, and peace, but then, on the other hand, radically acts to the contrary by allowing or tolerating a variety of ways in which human life is devalued and violated, especially where it is weak or marginalized."[29]

The Apostolic Exhortation *Evangelii Nuntiandi*, for its part, is very closely linked with development, given that, in Paul VI's words,

---

[27] Cf. nos. 8–9: *AAS* 60 (1968), 485–487; Benedict XVI, *Address to the Participants at the International Congress Promoted by the Pontifical Lateran University on the Fortieth Anniversary of Paul VI's Encyclical "Humanae Vitae"*, 10 May 2008.

[28] Cf. Encyclical Letter *Evangelium Vitae* (25 March 1995), 93: *AAS* 87 (1995), 507–508.

[29] *Ibid.*, 101: *loc. cit.*, 516–518.

"evangelization would not be complete if it did not take account of the unceasing interplay of the Gospel and of man's concrete life, both personal and social."[30] "Between evangelization and human advancement—development and liberation—there are in fact profound links":[31] on the basis of this insight, Paul VI clearly presented the relationship between the proclamation of Christ and the advancement of the individual in society. *Testimony to Christ's charity, through works of justice, peace, and development, is part and parcel of evangelization,* because Jesus Christ, who loves us, is concerned with the whole person. These important teachings form the basis for the missionary aspect[32] of the Church's social doctrine, which is an essential element of evangelization.[33] The Church's social doctrine proclaims and bears witness to faith. It is an instrument and an indispensable setting for formation in faith.

16. In *Populorum Progressio*, Paul VI taught that progress, in its origin and essence, is first and

---

[30] No. 29: *AAS* 68 (1976), 25.

[31] *Ibid.*, 31: *loc. cit.*, 26.

[32] Cf. John Paul II, Encyclical Letter *Sollicitudo Rei Socialis*, 41: *loc. cit.*, 570–572.

[33] Cf. *ibid.*; *idem*, Encyclical Letter *Centesimus Annus*, 5, 54: *loc. cit.*, 799, 859–860.

foremost a *vocation*: "in the design of God, every man is called upon to develop and fulfill himself, for every life is a vocation." [34] This is what gives legitimacy to the Church's involvement in the whole question of development. If development were concerned with merely technical aspects of human life, and not with the meaning of man's pilgrimage through history in company with his fellow human beings, nor with identifying the goal of that journey, then the Church would not be entitled to speak on it. Paul VI, like Leo XIII before him in *Rerum Novarum*,[35] knew that he was carrying out a duty proper to his office by shedding the light of the Gospel on the social questions of his time.[36]

To regard *development as a vocation* is to recognize, on the one hand, that it derives from a transcendent call and, on the other hand, that it is incapable, on its own, of supplying its ultimate meaning. Not without reason the word

---

[34] No. 15: *loc. cit.*, 265.

[35] Cf. *ibid.*, 2: *loc. cit.*, 258; Leo XIII, Encyclical Letter *Rerum Novarum* (15 May 1891): *Leonis XIII P.M. Acta*, XI, Romae 1892, 97–144; John Paul II, Encyclical Letter *Sollicitudo Rei Socialis*, 8: *loc. cit.*, 519–520; *idem*, Encyclical Letter *Centesimus Annus*, 5: *loc. cit.*, 799.

[36] Cf. Encyclical Letter *Populorum Progressio*, 2, 13: *loc. cit.*, 258, 263–264.

"vocation" is also found in another passage of the Encyclical, where we read: "There is no true humanism but that which is open to the Absolute and is conscious of a vocation which gives human life its true meaning." [37] This vision of development is at the heart of *Populorum Progressio*, and it lies behind all Paul VI's reflections on freedom, on truth, and on charity in development. It is also the principal reason why that Encyclical is still timely in our day.

17. A vocation is a call that requires a free and responsible answer. *Integral human development presupposes the responsible freedom* of the individual and of peoples: no structure can guarantee this development over and above human responsibility. The "types of messianism which give promises but create illusions" [38] always build their case on a denial of the transcendent dimension of development, in the conviction that it lies entirely at their disposal. This false security becomes a weakness, because it involves reducing man to subservience, to a mere means for development, while the humility of those who accept a vocation is transformed into true

[37] *Ibid.*, 42: *loc. cit.*, 278.
[38] *Ibid.*, 11: *loc. cit.*, 262; cf. John Paul II, Encyclical Letter *Centesimus Annus*, 25: *loc. cit.*, 822–824.

autonomy, because it sets them free. Paul VI
was in no doubt that obstacles and forms of
conditioning hold up development, but he was
also certain that "each one remains, whatever
be these influences affecting him, the principal agent of his own success or failure." [39] This
freedom concerns the type of development we
are considering, but it also affects situations of
underdevelopment which are not due to chance
or historical necessity but are attributable to
human responsibility. This is why "the peoples in hunger are making a dramatic appeal
to the peoples blessed with abundance." [40] This
too is a vocation, a call addressed by free subjects to other free subjects in favor of an
assumption of shared responsibility. Paul VI had
a keen sense of the importance of economic
structures and institutions, but he had an equally
clear sense of their nature as instruments of
human freedom. Only when it is free can development be integrally human; only in a climate of responsible freedom can it grow in a
satisfactory manner.

18. Besides requiring freedom, *integral human
development as a vocation also demands respect for*

---

[39] Encyclical Letter *Populorum Progressio*, 15: *loc. cit.*, 265.
[40] *Ibid.*, 3: *loc. cit.*, 258.

its truth. The vocation to progress drives us to "do more, know more, and have more in order to be more".[41] But herein lies the problem: what does it mean "to be more"? Paul VI answers the question by indicating the essential quality of "authentic" development: it must be "integral, that is, it has to promote the good of every man and of the whole man".[42] Amid the various competing anthropological visions put forward in today's society, even more so than in Paul VI's time, the Christian vision has the particular characteristic of asserting and justifying the unconditional value of the human person and the meaning of his growth. The Christian vocation to development helps to promote the advancement of all men and of the whole man. As Paul VI wrote: "What we hold important is man, each man and each group of men, and we even include the whole of humanity."[43] In promoting development, the Christian faith does not rely on privilege or positions of power or even on the merits of Christians (even though these existed and continue to

---

[41] *Ibid.*, 6: *loc. cit.*, 260.

[42] *Ibid.*, 14: *loc. cit.*, 264.

[43] *Ibid.*; cf. John Paul II, Encyclical Letter *Centesimus Annus*, 53–62: *loc. cit.*, 859–867; *idem*, Encyclical Letter *Redemptor Hominis* (4 March 1979), 13–14: *AAS* 71 (1979), 282–286.

exist alongside their natural limitations),[44] but only on Christ, to whom every authentic vocation to integral human development must be directed. *The Gospel is fundamental for development*, because in the Gospel, Christ, "in the very revelation of the mystery of the Father and of his love, fully reveals humanity to itself".[45] Taught by her Lord, the Church examines the signs of the times and interprets them, offering the world "what she possesses as her characteristic attribute: a global vision of man and of the human race".[46] Precisely because God gives a resounding "yes" to man,[47] man cannot fail to open himself to the divine vocation to pursue his own development. The truth of development consists in its completeness: if it does not involve the whole man and every man, it is not true development. This is the central message of *Populorum Progressio*, valid for today and for all time. Integral human development on the natural plane, as a response to a vocation from God

---

[44] Cf. Paul VI, Encyclical Letter *Populorum Progressio*, 12: *loc. cit.*, 262–263.

[45] Second Vatican Ecumenical Council, Pastoral Constitution on the Church in the Modern World *Gaudium et Spes*, 22.

[46] Paul VI, Encyclical Letter *Populorum Progressio*, 13: *loc. cit.*, 263–264.

[47] Cf. Benedict XVI, *Address to the Participants in the Fourth National Congress of the Church in Italy*, Verona, 19 October 2006.

the Creator,[48] demands self-fulfillment in a "transcendent humanism which gives [to man] his greatest possible perfection: this is the highest goal of personal development."[49] The Christian vocation to this development therefore applies to both the natural plane and the supernatural plane; which is why, "when God is eclipsed, our ability to recognize the natural order, purpose, and the 'good' begins to wane."[50]

19. Finally, the vision of development as a vocation brings with it the *central place of charity within that development*. Paul VI, in his Encyclical Letter *Populorum Progressio*, pointed out that the causes of underdevelopment are not primarily of the material order. He invited us to search for them in other dimensions of the human person: first of all, in the will, which often neglects the duties of solidarity; secondly, in thinking, which does not always give proper direction to the will. Hence, in the pursuit of development, there is a need for "the deep thought and reflection of wise

---

[48] Cf. Paul VI, Encyclical Letter *Populorum Progressio*, 16: *loc. cit.*, 265.

[49] *Ibid.*

[50] Benedict XVI, *Address to Young People at Barangaroo*, Sydney, 17 July 2008.

men in search of a new humanism which will
enable modern man to find himself anew".[51]
But that is not all. Underdevelopment has an
even more important cause than lack of deep
thought: it is "the lack of brotherhood among
individuals and peoples".[52] Will it ever be possible to obtain this brotherhood by human
effort alone? As society becomes ever more
globalized, it makes us neighbors but does not
make us brothers. Reason, by itself, is capable of grasping the equality between men and
of giving stability to their civic coexistence,
but it cannot establish fraternity. This origi-
nates in a transcendent vocation from God
the Father, who loved us first, teaching us
through the Son what fraternal charity is. Paul
VI, presenting the various levels in the process of human development, placed at the summit, after mentioning faith, "unity in the
charity of Christ, who calls us all to share as
sons in the life of the living God, the Father
of all".[53]

20. These perspectives, which *Populorum Progressio* opens up, remain fundamental for giving

---

[51] Paul VI, Encyclical Letter *Populorum Progressio*, 20: *loc. cit.*, 267.
[52] *Ibid.*, 66: *loc. cit.*, 289–290.
[53] *Ibid.*, 21: *loc. cit.*, 267–268.

breathing-space and direction to our commitment for the development of peoples. Moreover, *Populorum Progressio* repeatedly underlines
the *urgent need for reform*,[54] and in the face of great
problems of injustice in the development of peoples, it calls for courageous action to be taken
without delay. This *urgency is also a consequence
of charity in truth*. It is Christ's charity that drives
us on: *"caritas Christi urget nos"* (*2 Cor* 5:14). The
urgency is inscribed not only in things; it is
derived, not solely from the rapid succession of
events and problems, but also from the very matter that is at stake: the establishment of authentic fraternity.

The importance of this goal is such as to
demand our openness to understand it in depth
and to mobilize ourselves at the level of the
"heart", so as to ensure that current economic
and social processes evolve towards fully human
outcomes.

---

[54] Cf. nos. 3, 29, 32: *loc. cit.*, 258, 272, 273.

CHAPTER TWO

Human Development in Our Time

21. Paul VI had an *articulated vision of develop-ment*. He understood the term to indicate the goal of rescuing peoples, first and foremost, from hunger, deprivation, endemic diseases, and illiteracy. From the economic point of view, this meant their active participation, on equal terms, in the international economic process; from the social point of view, it meant their evolution into educated societies marked by sol-idarity; from the political point of view, it meant the consolidation of democratic regimes capa-ble of ensuring freedom and peace. After so many years, as we observe with concern the developments and perspectives of the succes-sion of crises that afflict the world today, *we ask to what extent Paul VI's expectations have been fulfilled* by the model of development adopted in recent decades. We recognize, therefore, that the Church had good reason to be concerned about the capacity of a purely technological society to set realistic goals and to make good use of the instruments at its disposal. Profit is useful if it serves as a means towards an end that provides a sense both of how to produce

it and of how to make good use of it. Once profit becomes the exclusive goal, if it is produced by improper means and without the common good as its ultimate end, it risks destroying wealth and creating poverty. The economic development that Paul VI hoped to see was meant to produce real growth, of benefit to everyone and genuinely sustainable. It is true that growth has taken place, and it continues to be a positive factor that has lifted billions of people out of misery—recently it has given many countries the possibility of becoming effective players in international politics. Yet it must be acknowledged that this same economic growth has been and continues to be weighed down by *malfunctions and dramatic problems*, highlighted even further by the current crisis. This presents us with choices that cannot be postponed concerning nothing less than the destiny of man, who, moreover, cannot prescind from his nature. The technical forces in play, the global interrelations, the damaging effects on the real economy of badly managed and largely speculative financial dealing, large-scale migration of peoples, often provoked by some particular circumstance and then given insufficient attention, the unregulated exploitation of the earth's resources: all this leads us today to reflect on the measures that would be necessary to provide a solution to problems that are not only new in comparison to those addressed by Pope Paul VI, but also, and above all, of decisive impact upon the present and future good of humanity. The different aspects of the crisis, its solutions, and any new development that the future may bring are increasingly interconnected; they imply one another; they require new efforts of holistic understanding and a *new humanistic synthesis*. The complexity and gravity of the present economic situation rightly cause us concern, but we must adopt a realistic attitude as we take up with confidence and hope the new responsibilities to which we are called by the prospect of a world in need of profound cultural renewal, a world that needs to rediscover fundamental values on which to build a better future. The current crisis obliges us to re-plan our journey, to set ourselves new rules and to discover new forms of commitment, to build on positive experiences and to reject negative ones. The crisis thus becomes *an opportunity for discernment in which to shape a new vision for the future*. In this spirit, with confidence rather than resignation, it is appropriate to address the difficulties of the present time.

22. Today the picture of development has *many overlapping layers*. The actors and the causes in

both underdevelopment and development are manifold; the faults and the merits are differentiated. This fact should prompt us to liberate ourselves from ideologies, which often oversimplify reality in artificial ways, and it should lead us to examine objectively the full human dimension of the problems. As John Paul II has already observed, the demarcation line between rich and poor countries is no longer as clear as it was at the time of *Populorum Progressio.*[55] *The world's wealth is growing in absolute terms, but inequalities are on the increase.* In rich countries, new sectors of society are succumbing to poverty, and new forms of poverty are emerging. In poorer areas, some groups enjoy a sort of "superdevelopment" of a wasteful and consumerist kind which forms an unacceptable contrast with the ongoing situations of dehumanizing deprivation. "The scandal of glaring inequalities"[56] continues. Corruption and illegality are unfortunately evident in the conduct of the economic and political class in rich countries, both old and new, as well as in poor ones. Among those who sometimes fail to respect the human rights of workers are large multinational companies as

---

[55] Cf. Encyclical Letter *Sollicitudo Rei Socialis*, 28: *loc. cit.*, 548–550.
[56] Paul VI, Encyclical Letter *Populorum Progressio*, 9: *loc. cit.*, 261–262.

well as local producers. International aid has often been diverted from its proper ends through irresponsible actions both within the chain of donors and within that of the beneficiaries. Similarly, in the context of immaterial or cultural causes of development and underdevelopment, we find these same patterns of responsibility reproduced. On the part of rich countries, there is excessive zeal for protecting knowledge through an unduly rigid assertion of the right to intellectual property, especially in the field of health care. At the same time, in some poor countries, cultural models and social norms of behavior persist which hinder the process of development.

23. Many areas of the globe today have evolved considerably, albeit in problematical and disparate ways, thereby taking their place among the great powers destined to play important roles in the future. Yet it should be stressed that *progress of a merely economic and technological kind is insufficient*. Development needs above all to be true and integral. The mere fact of emerging from economic backwardness, though positive in itself, does not resolve the complex issues of human advancement either for the countries that are spearheading such progress or for those that are already economically developed or even for those

that are still poor, which can suffer not just through old forms of exploitation, but also from the negative consequences of a growth that is marked by irregularities and imbalances.

After the collapse of the economic and political systems of the Communist countries of Eastern Europe and the end of the so-called *opposing blocs,* a complete re-examination of development was needed. Pope John Paul II called for it when in 1987 he pointed to the existence of these blocs as one of the principal causes of underdevelopment,[57] inasmuch as politics withdrew resources from the economy and from the culture, and ideology inhibited freedom. Moreover, in 1991, after the events of 1989, he asked that, in view of the ending of the blocs, there should be a comprehensive new plan for development, not only in those countries, but also in the West and in those parts of the world that were in the process of evolving.[58] This has been achieved only in part, and it is still a real duty that needs to be discharged, perhaps by means of the choices that

---

[57] Cf. Encyclical Letter *Sollicitudo Rei Socialis,* 20: *loc. cit.,* 536–537.

[58] Cf. John Paul II, Encyclical Letter *Centesimus Annus,* 22–29: *loc. cit.,* 819–830.

are necessary to overcome current economic problems.

24. The world that Paul VI had before him— even though society had already evolved to such an extent that he could speak of social issues in global terms—was still far less integrated than today's world. Economic activity and the political process were both largely conducted within the same geographical area and could therefore feed off one another. Production took place predominantly within national boundaries, and financial investments had somewhat limited circulation outside the country, so that the politics of many States could still determine the priorities of the economy and to some degree govern its performance using the instruments at their disposal. Hence *Populorum Progressio* assigned a central, albeit not exclusive, role to "public authorities".[59]

In our own day, the State finds itself having to address the limitations to its sovereignty imposed by the new context of international trade and finance, which is characterized by increasing mobility both of financial capital and means of production, material and immaterial. This

---

[59] Cf. nos. 23, 33: *loc. cit.*, 268–269, 273–274.

new context has altered the political power of States.

Today, as we take to heart the lessons of the current economic crisis, which sees the State's *public authorities* directly involved in correcting errors and malfunctions, it seems more realistic to *re-evaluate their role* and their powers, which need to be prudently reviewed and remodeled so as to enable them, perhaps through new forms of engagement, to address the challenges of today's world. Once the role of public authorities has been more clearly defined, one could foresee an increase in the new forms of political participation, nationally and internationally, that have come about through the activity of organizations operating in civil society; in this way it is to be hoped that the citizens' interest and participation in the *res publica* will become more deeply rooted.

25. From the social point of view, systems of protection and welfare, already present in many countries in Paul VI's day, are finding it hard and could find it even harder in the future to pursue their goals of true social justice in today's profoundly changed environment. The global market has stimulated first and foremost, on the

part of rich countries, a search for areas in which to outsource production at low cost with a view to reducing the prices of many goods, increasing purchasing power, and thus accelerating the rate of development in terms of greater availability of consumer goods for the domestic market. Consequently, the market has prompted new forms of competition between States as they seek to attract foreign businesses to set up production centers by means of a variety of instruments, including favorable fiscal regimes and deregulation of the labor market. These processes have led to a *downsizing of social security systems* as the price to be paid for seeking greater competitive advantage in the global market, with consequent grave danger for the rights of workers, for fundamental human rights, and for the solidarity associated with the traditional forms of the social State. Systems of social security can lose the capacity to carry out their task, both in emerging countries and in those that were among the earliest to develop as well as in poor countries. Here budgetary policies, with cuts in social spending often made under pressure from international financial institutions, can leave citizens powerless in the face of old and new risks; such powerlessness is increased by the lack of effective protection on the part of workers' associations. Through the combination of social and economic change, *trade union organizations* experience greater difficulty in carrying out their task of representing the interests of workers, partly because governments, for reasons of economic utility, often limit the freedom or the negotiating capacity of labor unions. Hence traditional networks of solidarity have more and more obstacles to overcome. The repeated calls issued within the Church's social doctrine, beginning with *Rerum Novarum*,[60] for the promotion of workers' associations that can defend their rights must therefore be honored today even more than in the past as a prompt and far-sighted response to the urgent need for new forms of cooperation at the international level as well as the local level.

The *mobility of labor*, associated with a climate of deregulation, is an important phenomenon with certain positive aspects, because it can stimulate wealth production and cultural exchange. Nevertheless, uncertainty over working conditions caused by mobility and deregulation, when it becomes endemic, tends to create new forms of psychological instability, giving rise to difficulty in forging coherent life-plans, including that of marriage. This leads

---

[60] Cf. *loc. cit.*, 135.

47

to situations of human decline, to say nothing
of the waste of social resources. In comparison with the casualties of industrial society in
the past, unemployment today provokes new
forms of economic marginalization, and the
current crisis can only make this situation worse.
Being out of work or dependent on public or
private assistance for a prolonged period under-
mines the freedom and creativity of the person and his family and social relationships,
causing great psychological and spiritual suffering. I would like to remind everyone, especially governments engaged in boosting the
world's economic and social assets, that the *primary capital to be safeguarded and valued is man,
the human person in his or her integrity*: "Man is
the source, the focus, and the aim of all economic and social life." [61]

26. On the cultural plane, compared with Paul
VI's day, the difference is even more marked.
At that time cultures were relatively well
defined and had greater opportunity to defend
themselves against attempts to merge them into
one. Today the possibilities of *interaction between
cultures* have increased significantly, giving rise

---

[61] Second Vatican Ecumenical Council, Pastoral Constitution on
the Church in the Modern World *Gaudium et Spes*, 63.

to new openings for intercultural dialogue: a
dialogue that, if it is to be effective, has to
set out from a deep-seated knowledge of the
specific identity of the various dialogue part-
ners. Let it not be forgotten that the increased
commercialization of cultural exchange today
leads to a twofold danger. First, one may
observe a *cultural eclecticism* that is often assumed
uncritically: cultures are simply placed alongside one another and viewed as substantially
equivalent and interchangeable. This easily
yields to a relativism that does not serve true
intercultural dialogue; on the social plane, cultural relativism has the effect that cultural
groups coexist side by side but remain separate, with no authentic dialogue and, therefore, with no true integration. Secondly, the
opposite danger exists, that of *cultural leveling*
and indiscriminate acceptance of types of conduct and lifestyles. In this way one loses sight
of the profound significance of the culture of
different nations, of the traditions of the various peoples, by which the individual defines
himself in relation to life's fundamental questions.[62] What eclecticism and cultural leveling have in common is the separation of

---

[62] Cf. John Paul II, Encyclical Letter *Centesimus Annus*, 24: *loc. cit.*, 821–822.

49

culture from human nature. Thus, cultures can no longer define themselves within a nature that transcends them,[63] and man ends up being reduced to a mere cultural statistic. When this happens, humanity runs new risks of enslavement and manipulation.

27. Life in many poor countries is still extremely insecure as a consequence of food shortages, and the situation could become worse: *hunger* still reaps enormous numbers of victims among those who, like Lazarus, are not permitted to take their place at the rich man's table, contrary to the hopes expressed by Paul VI.[64] *Feed the hungry* (cf. *Mt* 25:35, 37, 42) is an ethical imperative for the universal Church, as she responds to the teachings of her Founder, the Lord Jesus, concerning solidarity and the sharing of goods. Moreover, the elimination of world hunger has also, in the global era, become a requirement for safeguarding the peace and stability of the planet. Hunger is not so much dependent on

---

[63] Cf. John Paul II, Encyclical Letter *Veritatis Splendor* (6 August 1993), 33, 46, 51: *AAS* 85 (1993), 1160, 1169–1171, 1174–1175; *idem, Address to the Assembly of the United Nations*, 5 October 1995, 3.

[64] Cf. Encyclical Letter *Populorum Progressio*, 47: *loc. cit.*, 280–281; John Paul II, Encyclical Letter *Sollicitudo Rei Socialis*, 42: *loc. cit.*, 572–574.

a lack of material things as on a shortage of social resources, the most important of which are institutional. What is missing, in other words, is a network of economic institutions capable of guaranteeing regular access to sufficient food and water for nutritional needs and also capable of addressing the primary needs and necessities ensuing from genuine food crises, whether due to natural causes or political irresponsibility, nationally and internationally. The problem of food insecurity needs to be addressed within a long-term perspective, eliminating the structural causes that give rise to it and promoting the agricultural development of poorer countries. This can be done by investing in rural infrastructures, irrigation systems, transport, organization of markets, and in the development and dissemination of agricultural technology that can make the best use of the human, natural, and socioeconomic resources that are more readily available at the local level, while guaranteeing their sustainability over the long term as well. All this needs to be accomplished with the involvement of local communities in choices and decisions that affect the use of agricultural land. In this perspective, it could be useful to consider the new possibilities that are opening up through proper use of traditional as well as innovative farming techniques, always assuming that these have been judged, after sufficient testing, to be appropriate, respectful of the environment, and attentive to the needs of the most deprived peoples. At the same time, the question of equitable agrarian reform in developing countries should not be ignored. The right to food, like the right to water, has an important place within the pursuit of other rights, beginning with the fundamental right to life. It is therefore necessary to cultivate a public conscience that considers *food and access to water as universal rights of all human beings, without distinction or discrimination.*[65] It is important, moreover, to emphasize that solidarity with poor countries in the process of development can point towards a solution of the current global crisis, as politicians and directors of international institutions have begun to sense in recent times. Through support for economically poor countries by means of financial plans inspired by solidarity—so that these countries can take steps to satisfy their own citizens' demand for consumer goods and for development—not only can true economic growth be generated, but a contribution can

[65] Cf. Benedict XVI, *Message for the 2007 World Food Day: AAS* 99 (2007), 933–935.

be made towards sustaining the productive capacities of rich countries that risk being compromised by the crisis.

28. One of the most striking aspects of development in the present day is the important question of *respect for life*, which cannot in any way be detached from questions concerning the development of peoples. It is an aspect which has acquired increasing prominence in recent times, obliging us to broaden our concept of poverty[66] and underdevelopment to include questions connected with the acceptance of life, especially in cases where it is impeded in a variety of ways.

Not only does the situation of poverty still provoke high rates of infant mortality in many regions, but some parts of the world still experience practices of demographic control on the part of governments that often promote contraception and even go so far as to impose abortion. In economically developed countries, legislation contrary to life is very widespread, and it has already shaped moral attitudes and praxis, contributing to the spread of an anti-birth

---

[66] Cf. John Paul II, Encyclical Letter *Evangelium Vitae*, 18, 59, 63–64: loc. cit., 419–421, 467–468, 472–475.

mentality; frequent attempts are made to export this mentality to other States as if it were a form of cultural progress.

Some non-governmental organizations work actively to spread abortion, at times promoting the practice of sterilization in poor countries, in some cases not even informing the women concerned. Moreover, there is reason to suspect that development aid is sometimes linked to specific health-care policies which *de facto* involve the imposition of strong birth control measures. Further grounds for concern are laws permitting euthanasia as well as pressure from lobby groups, nationally and internationally, in favor of its juridical recognition.

Openness to life is at the center of true development. When a society moves towards the denial or suppression of life, it ends up no longer finding the necessary motivation and energy to strive for man's true good. If personal and social sensitivity towards the acceptance of a new life is lost, then other forms of acceptance that are valuable for society also wither away.[67] The acceptance of life strengthens moral fiber and makes people capable of mutual help. By cultivating

---

[67] Cf. Benedict XVI, *Message for the 2007 World Day of Peace*, 5.

openness to life, wealthy peoples can better understand the needs of poor ones, they can avoid employing huge economic and intellectual resources to satisfy the selfish desires of their own citizens, and instead, they can promote virtuous action within the perspective of production that is morally sound and marked by solidarity, respecting the fundamental right to life of every people and every individual.

29. There is another aspect of modern life that is very closely connected to development: the denial of the *right to religious freedom*. I am not referring simply to the struggles and conflicts that continue to be fought in the world for religious motives, even if at times the religious motive is merely a cover for other reasons, such as the desire for domination and wealth. Today, in fact, people frequently kill in the holy name of God, as both my predecessor John Paul II and I myself have often publicly acknowledged and lamented.[68] Violence puts the brakes on authentic development and impedes the evolution of

---

[68] Cf. John Paul II, *Message for the 2002 World Day of Peace*, 4–7, 12–15: *AAS* 94 (2002), 134–136, 138–140; *idem, Message for the 2004 World Day of Peace*, 8: *AAS* 96 (2004), 119; *idem, Message for the 2005 World Day of Peace*, 4: *AAS* 97 (2005), 177–178; Benedict XVI, *Message for the 2006 World Day of Peace*, 9–10: *AAS* 98 (2006), 60–61; *idem, Message for the 2007 World Day of Peace*, 5, 14: *loc. cit.*, 778, 782–783.

peoples towards greater socioeconomic and spiritual well-being. This applies especially to terrorism motivated by fundamentalism,[69] which generates grief, destruction, and death, obstructs dialogue between nations, and diverts extensive resources from their peaceful and civil uses.

Yet it should be added that, as well as religious fanaticism that in some contexts impedes the exercise of the right to religious freedom, so too the deliberate promotion of religious indifference or practical atheism on the part of many countries obstructs the requirements for the development of peoples, depriving them of spiritual and human resources. God is *the guarantor of man's true development*, inasmuch as, having created him in his image, he also establishes the transcendent dignity of men and women and feeds their innate yearning to "be more". Man is not a lost atom in a random universe:[70] he is God's creature, whom God chose to endow with an immortal soul and whom he has always loved. If man were merely the fruit of either chance or necessity, or if

---

[69] Cf. John Paul II, *Message for the 2002 World Day of Peace*, 6: *loc. cit.*, 135; Benedict XVI, *Message for the 2006 World Day of Peace*, 9–10: *loc. cit.*, 60–61.

[70] Cf. Benedict XVI, *Homily at Mass*, Islinger Feld, Regensburg, 12 September 2006.

he had to lower his aspirations to the limited horizon of the world in which he lives, if all reality were merely history and culture and man did not possess a nature destined to transcend itself in a supernatural life, then one could speak of growth, or evolution, but not development. When the State promotes, teaches, or actually imposes forms of practical atheism, it deprives its citizens of the moral and spiritual strength that is indispensable for attaining integral human development, and it impedes them from moving forward with renewed dynamism as they strive to offer a more generous human response to divine love.[71] In the context of cultural, commercial, or political relations, it also sometimes happens that economically developed or emerging countries export this reductive vision of the person and his destiny to poor countries. This is the damage that "superdevelopment"[72] causes to authentic development when it is accompanied by "moral underdevelopment".[73]

---

[71] Cf. Benedict XVI, Encyclical Letter *Deus Caritas Est*, 1: *loc. cit.*, 217–218.

[72] John Paul II, Encyclical Letter *Sollicitudo Rei Socialis*, 28: *loc. cit.*, 548–550.

[73] Paul VI, Encyclical Letter *Populorum Progressio*, 19: *loc. cit.*, 266–267.

30. In this context, the theme of integral human development takes on an even broader range of meanings: the correlation between its multiple elements requires a commitment to *foster the interaction of the different levels of human knowledge* in order to promote the authentic development of peoples. Often it is thought that development, or the socioeconomic measures that go with it, merely require to be implemented through joint action. This joint action, however, needs to be given direction, because "all social action involves a doctrine." [74] In view of the complexity of the issues, it is obvious that the various disciplines have to work together through an orderly interdisciplinary exchange. Charity does not exclude knowledge, but rather it requires, promotes, and animates it from within. Knowledge is never purely the work of the intellect. It can certainly be reduced to calculation and experiment, but if it aspires to be wisdom capable of directing man in the light of his first beginnings and his final ends, it must be "seasoned" with the "salt" of charity. Deeds without knowledge are blind, and knowledge without love is sterile. Indeed, "the individual who is animated by true charity labors

---

[74] *Ibid.*, 39: *loc. cit.*, 276–277.

skillfully to discover the causes of misery, to find the means to combat it, to overcome it resolutely."[75] Faced with the phenomena that lie before us, charity in truth requires first of all that we know and understand, acknowledging and respecting the specific competence of every level of knowledge. Charity is not an added extra, like an appendix to work already concluded in each of the various disciplines: it engages them in dialogue from the very beginning. The demands of love do not contradict those of reason. Human knowledge is insufficient, and the conclusions of science cannot indicate by themselves the path towards integral human development. There is always a need to push further ahead: this is what is required by charity in truth.[76] Going beyond, however, never means prescinding from the conclusions of reason or contradicting its results. Intelligence and love are not in separate compartments: *love is rich in intelligence, and intelligence is full of love.*

31. This means that moral evaluation and scientific research must go hand in hand and that

---

[75] *Ibid.,* 75: *loc. cit.,* 293–294.

[76] Cf. Benedict XVI, Encyclical Letter *Deus Caritas Est,* 28: *loc. cit.,* 238–240.

charity must animate them in a harmonious interdisciplinary whole, marked by unity and distinction. The Church's social doctrine, which has *"an important interdisciplinary dimension"*,[77] can exercise, in this perspective, a function of extraordinary effectiveness. It allows faith, theology, metaphysics, and science to come together in a collaborative effort in the service of humanity. It is here above all that the Church's social doctrine displays its dimension of wisdom. Paul VI had seen clearly that among the causes of underdevelopment there is a lack of wisdom and reflection, a lack of thinking capable of formulating a guiding synthesis,[78] for which "a clear vision of all economic, social, cultural, and spiritual aspects"[79] is required. The excessive segmentation of knowledge,[80] the rejection of metaphysics by the human sciences,[81] the difficulties encountered by dialogue between science and theology are damaging not only to the development of knowledge, but also to the development of peoples, because these things make it

---

[77] John Paul II, Encyclical Letter *Centesimus Annus*, 59: *loc. cit.*, 864.

[78] Cf. Encyclical Letter *Populorum Progressio*, 40, 85: *loc. cit.*, 277, 298–299.

[79] *Ibid.*, 13: *loc. cit.*, 263–264.

[80] Cf. John Paul II, Encyclical Letter *Fides et Ratio* (14 September 1998), 85: *AAS* 91 (1999), 72–73.

[81] Cf. *ibid.*, 83: *loc. cit.*, 70–71.

harder to see the integral good of man in its various dimensions. The "broadening [of] our concept of reason and its application"[82] is indispensable if we are to succeed in adequately weighing all the elements involved in the question of development and in the solution of socio-economic problems.

32. The significant new elements in the picture of the development of peoples today in many cases demand *new solutions*. These need to be found together, respecting the laws proper to each element and in the light of an integral vision of man, reflecting the different aspects of the human person, contemplated through a lens purified by charity. Remarkable convergences and possible solutions will then come to light, without any fundamental component of human life being obscured.

The dignity of the individual and the demands of justice require, particularly today, that economic choices do not cause disparities in wealth to increase in an excessive and morally unacceptable manner[83] and that we continue to

---

[82] Benedict XVI, *Address at the University of Regensburg*, 12 September 2006.

[83] Cf. Paul VI, Encyclical Letter *Populorum Progressio*, 33: *loc. cit.*, 273–274.

prioritize the goal of access to steady employment for everyone. All things considered, this is also required by "economic logic". Through the systemic increase of social inequality, both within a single country and between the populations of different countries (i.e., the massive increase in relative poverty), not only does social cohesion suffer, thereby placing democracy at risk, but so too does the economy, through the progressive erosion of "social capital": the network of relationships of trust, dependability, and respect for rules, all of which are indispensable for any form of civil coexistence.

Economic science tells us that structural insecurity generates anti-productive attitudes wasteful of human resources, inasmuch as workers tend to adapt passively to automatic mechanisms rather than to release creativity. On this point too, there is a convergence between economic science and moral evaluation. *Human costs always include economic costs*, and economic dysfunctions always involve human costs.

It should be remembered that the reduction of cultures to the technological dimension, even if it favors short-term profits, in the long term impedes reciprocal enrichment and the dynamics of cooperation. It is important to distinguish between short- and long-term economic or sociological considerations. Lowering the level of protection accorded to the rights of workers or abandoning mechanisms of wealth redistribution in order to increase the country's international competitiveness hinders the achievement of lasting development. Moreover, the human consequences of current tendencies towards a short-term economy—sometimes very short-term—need to be carefully evaluated. This requires *further and deeper reflection on the meaning of the economy and its goals*[84] as well as a profound and far-sighted revision of the current model of development, so as to correct its dysfunctions and deviations. This is demanded, in any case, by the earth's state of ecological health; above all it is required by the cultural and moral crisis of man, the symptoms of which have been evident for some time all over the world.

33. More than forty years after *Populorum Progressio*, its basic theme, namely progress, *remains an open question*, made all the more acute and urgent by the current economic and financial crisis. If some areas of the globe with a history of poverty have experienced remarkable changes

---

[84] Cf. John Paul II, *Message for the 2000 World Day of Peace*, 15: *AAS* 92 (2000), 366.

in terms of their economic growth and their share in world production, other zones are still living in a situation of deprivation comparable to that which existed at the time of Paul VI, and in some cases one can even speak of a deterioration. It is significant that some of the causes of this situation were identified in *Populorum Progressio*, such as the high tariffs imposed by economically developed countries, which still make it difficult for the products of poor countries to gain a foothold in the markets of rich countries. Other causes, however, mentioned only in passing in the Encyclical, have since emerged with greater clarity. A case in point would be the evaluation of the process of decolonization, then at its height. Paul VI hoped to see the journey towards autonomy unfold freely and in peace. More than forty years later, we must acknowledge how difficult this journey has been, both because of new forms of colonialism and continued dependence on old and new foreign powers and because of grave irresponsibility within the very countries that have achieved independence.

The principal new feature has been the *explosion of worldwide interdependence*, commonly known as globalization. Paul VI had partially foreseen it, but the ferocious pace at which it has evolved could not have been anticipated. Originating within economically developed countries, this process by its nature has spread to include all economies. It has been the principal driving force behind the emergence from underdevelopment of whole regions, and in itself it represents a great opportunity. Nevertheless, without the guidance of charity in truth, this global force could cause unprecedented damage and create new divisions within the human family. Hence charity and truth confront us with an altogether new and creative challenge, one that is certainly vast and complex. It is about *broadening the scope of reason and making it capable of knowing and directing these powerful new forces*, animating them within the perspective of that "civilization of love" whose seed God has planted in every people, in every culture.

CHAPTER THREE

Fraternity, Economic Development, and Civil Society

34. *Charity in truth* places man before the astonishing experience of gift. Gratuitousness is present in our lives in many different forms, which often go unrecognized because of a purely consumerist and utilitarian view of life. The human being is made for gift, which expresses and makes present his transcendent dimension. Sometimes modern man is wrongly convinced that he is the sole author of himself, his life, and society. This is a presumption that follows from being selfishly closed in upon himself, and it is a consequence—to express it in faith terms—of *original sin*. The Church's wisdom has always pointed to the presence of original sin in social conditions and in the structure of society: "Ignorance of the fact that man has a wounded nature inclined to evil gives rise to serious errors in the areas of education, politics, social action, and morals." [85] In the list of areas where the

---

[85] *Catechism of the Catholic Church*, 407; cf. John Paul II, Encyclical Letter *Centesimus Annus*, 25: *loc. cit.*, 822–824.

pernicious effects of sin are evident, the economy has been included for some time now.
We have a clear proof of this at the present
time. The conviction that man is self-sufficient
and can successfully eliminate the evil present
in history by his own action alone has led
him to confuse happiness and salvation with
immanent forms of material prosperity and
social action. Then, the conviction that the
economy must be autonomous, that it must
be shielded from "influences" of a moral character, has led man to abuse the economic process in a thoroughly destructive way. In the
long term, these convictions have led to economic, social, and political systems that tram-
ple upon personal and social freedom and are
therefore unable to deliver the justice that they
promise. As I said in my Encyclical Letter *Spe
Salvi*, history is thereby deprived of *Christian
hope*,[86] deprived of a powerful social resource
at the service of integral human development,
sought in freedom and in justice. Hope encourages reason and gives it the strength to direct the
will.[87] It is already present in faith, indeed it is
called forth by faith. Charity in truth feeds on
hope and, at the same time, manifests it. As the

---

[86] Cf. no. 17: *AAS* 99 (2007), 1000.
[87] Cf. *ibid.*, 23: *loc. cit.*, 1004–1005.

absolutely gratuitous gift of God, hope bursts into our lives as something not due to us, something that transcends every law of justice. Gift by its nature goes beyond merit; its rule is that of superabundance. It takes first place in our souls as a sign of God's presence in us, a sign of what he expects from us. Truth—which is itself gift in the same way as charity—is greater than we are, as Saint Augustine teaches.[88] Likewise the truth of ourselves, of our personal conscience, is first of all *given* to us. In every cognitive process, truth is not something that we produce; it is always found, or better, received. Truth, like love, "is neither planned nor willed, but somehow imposes itself upon human beings".[89]

Because it is a gift received by everyone, charity in truth is a force that builds community; it brings all people together without imposing

---

[88] Saint Augustine expounds this teaching in detail in his dialogue on free will (*De libero arbitrio* II, 3, 8ff.). He indicates the existence within the human soul of an "internal sense". This sense consists in an act that is fulfilled outside the normal functions of reason, an act that is not the result of reflection, but is almost instinctive, through which reason, realizing its transient and fallible nature, admits the existence of something eternal, higher than itself, something absolutely true and certain. The name that Saint Augustine gives to this interior truth is at times the name of God (*Confessions* X, 24, 35; XII, 25, 35; *De libero arbitrio* II, 3, 8), more often that of Christ (*De magistro* 11:38; *Confessions* VII, 18, 24; XI, 2, 4).

[89] Benedict XVI, Encyclical Letter *Deus Caritas Est*, 3: *loc. cit.*, 219.

barriers or limits. The human community that we build by ourselves can never, purely by its own strength, be a fully fraternal community; nor can it overcome every division and become a truly universal community. The unity of the human race, a fraternal communion transcending every barrier, is called into being by the word of God-who-is-Love. In addressing this key question, we must make it clear, on the one hand, that the logic of gift does not exclude justice; nor does it merely sit alongside it as a second element added from without; on the other hand, economic, social, and political development, if it is to be authentically human, needs to make room for the *principle of gratuitousness* as an expression of fraternity.

35. In a climate of mutual trust, the *market* is the economic institution that permits encounter between persons, inasmuch as they are economic subjects who make use of contracts to regulate their relations as they exchange goods and services of equivalent value between them, in order to satisfy their needs and desires. The market is subject to the principles of so-called *commutative justice*, which regulates the relations of giving and receiving between parties to a transaction. But the social doctrine of the Church has unceasingly highlighted the importance of

distributive justice and *social justice* for the market
economy, not only because the market belongs
within a broader social and political context, but
also because of the wider network of relations
within which it operates. In fact, if the market
is governed solely by the principle of the equiv-
alence in value of exchanged goods, it cannot
produce the social cohesion that it requires in
order to function well. *Without internal forms of
solidarity and mutual trust, the market cannot completely fulfill its proper economic function.* And today
it is this trust which has ceased to exist, and
the loss of trust is a grave loss. It was timely
when Paul VI in *Populorum Progressio* insisted
that the economic system itself would benefit
from the wide-ranging practice of justice, inasmuch as the first to gain from the development of poor countries would be rich ones.[90]
According to the Pope, it was not just a matter of correcting dysfunctions through assistance. The poor are to be considered, not a
"burden",[91] but a resource, even from the
purely economic point of view. It is nevertheless erroneous to hold that the market economy has an inbuilt need for a quota of poverty

---

[90] Cf. no. 49: *loc. cit.*, 281.

[91] John Paul II, Encyclical Letter *Centesimus Annus*, 28: *loc. cit.*,
827–828.

and underdevelopment in order to function at its best. It is in the interests of the market to promote emancipation, but in order to do so effectively, it cannot rely only on itself, because it is not able to produce by itself something that lies outside its competence. It must draw its moral energies from other subjects that are capable of generating them.

36. Economic activity cannot solve all social problems through the simple application of *commercial logic*. This needs to be *directed towards the pursuit of the common good*, for which the political community in particular must also take responsibility. Therefore, it must be borne in mind that grave imbalances are produced when economic action, conceived merely as an engine for wealth creation, is detached from political action, conceived as a means for pursuing justice through redistribution.

The Church has always held that economic action is not to be regarded as something opposed to society. In and of itself, the market is not, and must not become, the place where the strong subdue the weak. Society does not have to protect itself from the market, as if the development of the latter were *ipso facto* to entail the death of authentically human relations. Admittedly, the market can be a negative force, not because it is so by nature, but because a certain ideology can make it so. It must be remembered that the market does not exist in the pure state. It is shaped by the cultural configurations which define it and give it direction. Economy and finance, as instruments, can be used badly when those at the helm are motivated by purely selfish ends. Instruments that are good in themselves can thereby be transformed into harmful ones. But it is man's darkened reason that produces these consequences, not the instrument *per se*. Therefore it is not the instrument that must be called to account, but individuals, their moral conscience, and their personal and social responsibility.

The Church's social doctrine holds that authentically human social relationships of friendship, solidarity, and reciprocity can also be conducted within economic activity, and not only outside it or "after" it. The economic sphere is neither ethically neutral nor inherently inhuman and opposed to society. It is part and parcel of human activity, and precisely because it is human, it must be structured and governed in an ethical manner.

The great challenge before us, accentuated by the problems of development in this global era and made even more urgent by the economic and financial crisis, is to demonstrate, in thinking and behavior, not only that traditional principles of social ethics like transparency, honesty, and responsibility cannot be ignored or attenuated, but also that in *commercial relationships* the *principle of gratuitousness* and the logic of gift as an expression of fraternity can and must *find their place within normal economic activity.* This is a human demand at the present time, but it is also demanded by economic logic. It is a demand both of charity and of truth.

37. The Church's social doctrine has always maintained that *justice must be applied to every phase of economic activity,* because this is always concerned with man and his needs. Locating resources, financing, production, consumption, and all the other phases in the economic cycle inevitably have moral implications. *Thus every economic decision has a moral consequence.* The social sciences and the direction taken by the contemporary economy point to the same conclusion. Perhaps at one time it was conceivable that first the creation of wealth could be entrusted to the economy, and then the task of distributing it could be assigned to politics. Today that would be more difficult, given that economic activity is no longer circumscribed

within territorial limits, while the authority of governments continues to be principally local. Hence the canons of justice must be respected from the outset, as the economic process unfolds, and not just afterwards or incidentally. Space also needs to be created within the market for economic activity carried out by subjects who freely choose to act according to principles other than those of pure profit, without sacrificing the production of economic value in the process. The many economic entities that draw their origin from religious and lay initiatives demonstrate that this is concretely possible.

In the global era, the economy is influenced by competitive models tied to cultures that differ greatly among themselves. The different forms of economic enterprise to which they give rise find their main point of encounter in commutative justice. *Economic life* undoubtedly requires *contracts* in order to regulate relations of exchange between goods of equivalent value. But it also needs *just laws* and *forms of redistribution* governed by politics, and what is more, it needs works redolent of the *spirit of gift*. The economy in the global era seems to privilege the former logic, that of contractual exchange, but directly or indirectly it also demonstrates its need for the other two: political logic and the logic of the unconditional gift.

38. My predecessor John Paul II drew attention to this question in *Centesimus Annus* when he spoke of the need for a system with three subjects: the *market*, the *State*, and *civil society*.[92] He saw civil society as the most natural setting for an *economy of gratuitousness* and fraternity, but he did not mean to deny it a place in the other two settings. Today we can say that economic life must be understood as a multi-layered phenomenon: in every one of these layers, to varying degrees and in ways specifically suited to each, the aspect of fraternal reciprocity must be present. In the global era, economic activity cannot prescind from gratuitousness, which fosters and disseminates solidarity and responsibility for justice and the common good among the different economic players. It is clearly a specific and profound form of economic democracy. Solidarity is first and foremost a sense of responsibility on the part of everyone with regard to everyone,[93] and it cannot therefore be merely delegated to the

---

[92] Cf. no. 35: *loc. cit.*, 836–838.
[93] Cf. John Paul II, Encyclical Letter *Sollicitudo Rei Socialis*, 38: *loc. cit.*, 565–566.

State. While in the past it was possible to argue that justice had to come first and gratuitousness could follow afterwards, as a complement, today it is clear that without gratuitousness, there can be no justice in the first place. What is needed, therefore, is a market that permits the free operation, in conditions of equal opportunity, of enterprises in pursuit of different institutional ends. Alongside profit-oriented private enterprise and the various types of public enterprise, there must be room for commercial entities based on mutualist principles and pursuing social ends to take root and express themselves. It is from their reciprocal encounter in the marketplace that one may expect hybrid forms of commercial behavior to emerge and, hence, an attentiveness to ways of *civilizing the economy*. Charity in truth, in this case, requires that shape and structure be given to those types of economic initiative which, without rejecting profit, aim at a higher goal than the mere logic of the exchange of equivalents, of profit as an end in itself.

39. Paul VI in *Populorum Progressio* called for the creation of *a model of market economy capable of including within its range all peoples and not just the better off*. He called for efforts to

build a more human world for all, a world in which "all will be able to give and receive, without one group making progress at the expense of the other."[94] In this way he was applying on a global scale the insights and aspirations contained in *Rerum Novarum*, written when, as a result of the Industrial Revolution, the idea was first proposed—somewhat ahead of its time—that the civil order, for its self-regulation, also needed intervention from the State for purposes of redistribution. Not only is this vision threatened today by the way in which markets and societies are opening up, but it is evidently insufficient to satisfy the demands of a fully humane economy. What the Church's social doctrine has always sustained, on the basis of its vision of man and society, is corroborated today by the dynamics of globalization.

When both the logic of the market and the logic of the State come to an agreement that each will continue to exercise a monopoly over its respective area of influence, in the long term much is lost: solidarity in relations between citizens, participation and adherence, actions of gratuitousness, all of which stand in contrast with *giving*

---

[94] No. 44: *loc. cit.*, 279.

in order to acquire (the logic of exchange) and *giving through duty* (the logic of public obligation, imposed by State law). In order to defeat underdevelopment, action is required not only on improving exchange-based transactions and implanting public welfare structures, but above all on gradually *increasing openness, in a world context, to forms of economic activity marked by quotas of gratuitousness and communion.* The exclusively binary model of market-plus-State is corrosive of society, while economic forms based on solidarity, which find their natural home in civil society without being restricted to it, build up society. The market of gratuitousness does not exist, and attitudes of gratuitousness cannot be established by law. Yet both the market and politics need individuals who are open to reciprocal gift.

40. Today's international economic scene, marked by grave deviations and failures, requires a *profoundly new way of understanding business enterprise.* Old models are disappearing, but promising new ones are taking shape on the horizon. Without doubt, one of the greatest risks for businesses is that they are almost exclusively answerable to their investors, thereby limiting their social value. Owing to their growth in scale and the need for more and more capital, it is

becoming increasingly rare for business enterprises to be in the hands of a stable director who feels responsible in the long term, not just the short term, for the life and the results of his company, and it is becoming increasingly rare for businesses to depend on a single territory. Moreover, the so-called outsourcing of production can weaken the company's sense of responsibility towards the stakeholders—namely, the workers, the suppliers, the consumers, the natural environment, and broader society—in favor of the shareholders, who are not tied to a specific geographical area and who therefore enjoy extraordinary mobility. Today's international capital market offers great freedom of action. Yet there is also increasing awareness of the need for greater *social responsibility* on the part of business. Even if the ethical considerations that currently inform debate on the social responsibility of the corporate world are not all acceptable from the perspective of the Church's social doctrine, there is nevertheless a growing conviction that *business management cannot concern itself only with the interests of the proprietors but must also assume responsibility for all the other stakeholders who contribute to the life of the business*: the workers, the clients, the suppliers of various elements of production, the community of reference. In recent years a new cosmopolitan class of *managers* has emerged, who are often answerable only to the shareholders generally consisting of anonymous funds which *de facto* determine their remuneration. By contrast, though, many far-sighted managers today are becoming increasingly aware of the profound links between their enterprise and the territory or territories in which it operates. Paul VI invited people to give serious attention to the damage that can be caused to one's home country by the transfer abroad of capital purely for personal advantage.[95] John Paul II taught that *investment always has moral as well as economic significance.*[96] All this—it should be stressed—is still valid today, despite the fact that the capital market has been significantly liberalized and modern technological thinking can suggest that investment is merely a technical act, not a human and ethical one. There is no reason to deny that a certain amount of capital can do good if invested abroad rather than at home. Yet the requirements of justice must be safeguarded, with due consideration for the way in which the capital was generated and the harm to individuals that will result if it is not used where it was produced.[97] What should be

---

[95] Cf. *ibid.,* 24: *loc. cit.,* 269.

[96] Cf. Encyclical Letter *Centesimus Annus,* 36: *loc. cit.,* 838–840.

[97] Cf. Paul VI, Encyclical Letter *Populorum Progressio,* 24: *loc. cit.,* 269.

avoided is a speculative *use of financial resources* that yields to the temptation of seeking only short-term profit, without regard for the long-term sustainability of the enterprise, its benefit to the real economy, and attention to the advancement, in suitable and appropriate ways, of further economic initiatives in countries in need of development. It is true that the export of investments and skills can benefit the populations of the receiving country. Labor and technical knowledge are a universal good. Yet it is not right to export these things merely for the sake of obtaining advantageous conditions or, worse, for purposes of exploitation, without making a real contribution to local society by helping to bring about a robust productive and social system, an essential factor for stable development.

41. In the context of this discussion, it is helpful to observe that *business enterprise* involves a *wide range of values*, becoming wider all the time. The continuing hegemony of the binary model of market-plus-State has accustomed us to think only in terms of the private business leader of a capitalistic bent, on the one hand, and the State director, on the other. In reality, business has to be understood in an articulated way. There are a number of reasons, of a meta-economic kind, for saying this. Business

activity has a human significance, prior to its professional one.[98] It is present in all work, understood as a personal action, an *"actus personae"*,[99] which is why every worker should have the chance to make his contribution knowing that in some way "he is working 'for himself'." [100] With good reason, Paul VI taught that "everyone who works is a creator." [101] It is in response to the needs and the dignity of the worker, as well as the needs of society, that there exist various types of business enterprise, over and above the simple distinction between "private" and "public". Each of them requires and expresses a specific business capacity. In order to construct an economy that will soon be in a position to serve the national and global common good, it is appropriate to take account of this broader significance of business activity. It favors cross-fertilization between different types of business activity, with shifting of competences from the "non-profit" world to the

---

[98] Cf. John Paul II, Encyclical Letter *Centesimus Annus*, 32: *loc. cit.*, 832–833; Paul VI, Encyclical Letter *Populorum Progressio*, 25: *loc. cit.*, 269–270.

[99] John Paul II, Encyclical Letter *Laborem Exercens*, 24: *loc. cit.*, 637–638.

[100] *Ibid.*, 15: *loc. cit.*, 616–618.

[101] Encyclical Letter *Populorum Progressio*, 27: *loc. cit.*, 271.

"profit" world and vice versa, from the public world to that of civil society, from advanced economies to developing countries.

"*Political authority*" also involves a *wide range of values*, which must not be overlooked in the process of constructing a new order of economic productivity, socially responsible and human in scale. As well as cultivating differentiated forms of business activity on the global plane, we must also promote a dispersed political authority, effective on different levels. The integrated economy of the present day does not make the role of States redundant, but rather it commits governments to greater collaboration with one another. Both wisdom and prudence suggest not being too precipitous in declaring the demise of the State. In terms of the resolution of the current crisis, the State's role seems destined to grow, as it regains many of its competences. In some nations, moreover, the construction or reconstruction of the State remains a key factor in their development. The focus of *international aid*, within a solidarity-based plan to resolve today's economic problems, should rather be on consolidating constitutional, juridical, and administrative systems in countries that do not yet fully enjoy these goods. Alongside economic aid, there needs to be aid directed towards reinforcing the guarantees proper to the *State of law*: a system of public order and effective imprisonment that respects human rights, truly democratic institutions. The State does not need to have identical characteristics everywhere: the support aimed at strengthening weak constitutional systems can easily be accompanied by the development of other political players, of a cultural, social, territorial, or religious nature, alongside the State. The articulation of political authority at the local, national, and international levels is one of the best ways of giving direction to the process of economic globalization. It is also the way to ensure that it does not actually undermine the foundations of democracy.

42. Sometimes *globalization* is viewed in fatalistic terms, as if the dynamics involved were the product of anonymous impersonal forces or structures independent of the human will.[102] In this regard it is useful to remember that while globalization should certainly be understood as a socioeconomic process, this is not its only dimension. Underneath the more visible process, humanity itself is becoming increasingly

---

[102] Cf. Congregation for the Doctrine of the Faith, Instruction on Christian Freedom and Liberation *Libertatis Conscientia* (22 March 1987), 74: *AAS* 79 (1987), 587.

interconnected; it is made up of individuals and peoples to whom this process should offer benefits and development[103] as they assume their respective responsibilities, singly and collectively. The breaking-down of borders is not simply a material fact: it is also a cultural event both in its causes and in its effects. If globalization is viewed from a deterministic standpoint, the criteria with which to evaluate and direct it are lost. As a human reality, it is the product of diverse cultural tendencies, which need to be subjected to a process of discernment. The truth of globalization as a process and its fundamental ethical criterion are given by the unity of the human family and its development towards what is good. Hence a sustained commitment is needed so as to *promote a person-based and community-oriented cultural process of worldwide integration that is open to transcendence.*

Despite some of its structural elements, which should be neither denied nor exaggerated, "globalization, *a priori*, is neither good nor bad. It will be what people make of it." [104] We should be,

---

[103] Cf. John Paul II, Interview published in the Catholic daily newspaper *La Croix*, 20 August 1997.

[104] John Paul II, *Address to the Pontifical Academy of Social Sciences*, 27 April 2001.

not its victims, but rather its protagonists, acting in the light of reason, guided by charity and truth. Blind opposition would be a mistaken and prejudiced attitude, incapable of recognizing the positive aspects of the process, with the consequent risk of missing the chance to take advantage of its many opportunities for development. The processes of globalization, suitably understood and directed, open up the unprecedented possibility of large-scale redistribution of wealth on a worldwide scale; if badly directed, however, they can lead to an increase in poverty and inequality and could even trigger a global crisis. It is necessary to *correct the malfunctions*, some of them serious, that cause new divisions between peoples and within peoples and also to ensure that the redistribution of wealth does not come about through the redistribution or increase of poverty: a real danger if the present situation were to be badly managed. For a long time it was thought that poor peoples should remain at a fixed stage of development and should be content to receive assistance from the philanthropy of developed peoples. Paul VI strongly opposed this mentality in *Populorum Progressio*. Today the material resources available for rescuing these peoples from poverty are potentially greater than before, but they have ended up largely in the hands of people from developed countries, who have benefited more from the liberalization that has occurred in the mobility of capital and labor. The worldwide diffusion of forms of prosperity should not therefore be held up by projects that are self-centered, protectionist, or at the service of private interests. Indeed, the involvement of emerging or developing countries allows us to manage the crisis better today. The transition inherent in the process of globalization presents great difficulties and dangers that can only be overcome if we are able to appropriate the underlying anthropological and ethical spirit that drives globalization towards the humanizing goal of solidarity. Unfortunately this spirit is often overwhelmed or suppressed by ethical and cultural considerations of an individualistic and utilitarian nature. Globalization is a multifaceted and complex phenomenon which must be grasped in the diversity and unity of all its different dimensions, including the theological dimension. In this way it will be possible to experience and to *steer the globalization of humanity in relational terms, in terms of communion and the sharing of goods.*

CHAPTER FOUR

The Development of People— Rights and Duties— The Environment

43. "The reality of human solidarity, which is a benefit for us, also imposes a duty." [105] Many people today would claim that they owe nothing to anyone, except to themselves. They are concerned only with their rights, and they often have great difficulty in taking responsibility for their own and other people's integral development. Hence it is important to call for a renewed reflection on how *rights presuppose duties, if they are not to become mere license.*[106] Nowadays we are witnessing a grave inconsistency. On the one hand, appeals are made to alleged rights, arbitrary and nonessential in nature, accompanied by the demand that they be recognized and promoted by public structures, while, on the other hand, elementary and basic rights remain unacknowledged

---

[105] Paul VI, Encyclical Letter *Populorum Progressio*, 17: *loc. cit.*, 265–266.
[106] Cf. John Paul II, *Message for the 2003 World Day of Peace*, 5: *AAS* 95 (2003), 343.

and are violated in much of the world.[107] A link has often been noted between claims to a "right to excess", and even to transgression and vice, within affluent societies and the lack of food, drinkable water, basic instruction, and elementary health care in areas of the under-developed world and on the outskirts of large metropolitan centers. The link consists in this: individual rights, when detached from a frame-work of duties which grants them their full meaning, can run wild, leading to an escala-tion of demands which is effectively unlim-ited and indiscriminate. An overemphasis on rights leads to a disregard for duties. Duties set a limit on rights because they point to the anthropological and ethical framework of which rights are a part, in this way ensuring that they do not become license. Duties thereby reinforce rights and call for their defense and promotion as a task to be under-taken in the service of the common good. Otherwise, if the only basis of human rights is to be found in the deliberations of an assem-bly of citizens, those rights can be changed at any time, and so the duty to respect and pursue them fades from the common consciousness. Governments and international

---

[107] Cf. *ibid.*

bodies can then lose sight of the objectivity and "inviolability" of rights. When this happens, the authentic development of peoples is endangered.[108] Such a way of thinking and acting compromises the authority of international bodies, especially in the eyes of those countries most in need of development. Indeed, the latter demand that the international community take up the duty of helping them to be "artisans of their own destiny",[109] that is, to take up duties of their own. *The sharing of reciprocal duties is a more powerful incentive to action than the mere assertion of rights.*

44. The notion of rights and duties in development must also take account of the problems associated with *population growth*. This is a very important aspect of authentic development, since it concerns the inalienable values of life and the family.[110] To consider population increase as the primary cause of underdevelopment is mistaken, even from an economic point of view. Suffice it to consider,

---

[108] Cf. Benedict XVI, *Message for the 2007 World Day of Peace*, 13: *loc. cit.*, 781–782.

[109] Paul VI, Encyclical Letter *Populorum Progressio*, 65: *loc. cit.*, 289.

[110] Cf. *ibid.*, 36–37: *loc. cit.*, 275–276.

on the one hand, the significant reduction in infant mortality and the rise in average life expectancy found in economically developed countries and, on the other hand, the signs of crisis observable in societies that are registering an alarming decline in their birth rate. Due attention must obviously be given to responsible procreation, which among other things has a positive contribution to make to integral human development. The Church, in her concern for man's authentic development, urges him to have full respect for human values in the exercise of his sexuality. It cannot be reduced merely to pleasure or entertainment; nor can sex education be reduced to technical instruction aimed solely at protecting the interested parties from possible disease or the "risk" of procreation. This would be to impoverish and disregard the deeper meaning of sexuality, a meaning which needs to be acknowledged and responsibly appropriated not only by individuals but also by the community. It is irresponsible to view sexuality merely as a source of pleasure and, likewise, to regulate it through strategies of mandatory birth control. In either case materialistic ideas and policies are at work, and individuals are ultimately subjected to various forms of violence. Against such policies, there is a need to defend the primary competence of the family in the area of sexuality,[111] as opposed to the State and its restrictive policies, and to ensure that parents are suitably prepared to undertake their responsibilities.

Morally responsible openness to life represents a rich social and economic resource. Populous nations have been able to emerge from poverty thanks not least to the size of their population and the talents of their people. On the other hand, formerly prosperous nations are presently passing through a phase of uncertainty and in some cases decline precisely because of their falling birth rates; this has become a crucial problem for highly affluent societies. The decline in births, falling at times beneath the so-called "replacement level", also puts a strain on social welfare systems, increases their cost, eats into savings and hence the financial resources needed for investment, reduces the availability of qualified laborers, and narrows the "brain pool" upon which nations can draw for their needs. Furthermore, smaller and at times miniscule families run the risk of impoverishing social relations and failing to ensure effective forms of solidarity. These situations are symptomatic

---

[111] Cf. *ibid.*, 37: *loc. cit.*, 275–276.

of scant confidence in the future and moral weariness. It is thus becoming a social and even economic necessity once more to hold up to future generations the beauty of marriage and the family and the fact that these institutions correspond to the deepest needs and dignity of the person. In view of this, States are called to *enact policies promoting the centrality and the integrity of the family* founded on marriage between a man and a woman, the primary vital cell of society,[112] and to assume responsibility for its economic and fiscal needs, while respecting its essentially relational character.

45. Striving to meet the deepest moral needs of the person also has important and beneficial repercussions at the level of economics. *The economy needs ethics in order to function correctly*—not any ethics whatsoever, but an ethics which is people-centered. Today we hear much talk of ethics in the world of economy, finance, and business. Research centers and seminars in business ethics are on the rise; the system of ethical certification is spreading throughout the developed world as part of the movement of ideas associated with the responsibilities of business

---

[112] Cf. Second Vatican Ecumenical Council, Decree on the Apostolate of Lay People *Apostolicam Actuositatem*, 11.

towards society. Banks are proposing "ethical" accounts and investment funds. "Ethical financing" is being developed, especially through micro-credit and, more generally, micro-finance. These processes are praiseworthy and deserve much support. Their positive effects are also being felt in the less developed areas of the world. It would be advisable, however, to develop a sound criterion of discernment, since the adjective "ethical" can be abused. When the word is used generically, it can lend itself to any number of interpretations, even to the point where it includes decisions and choices contrary to justice and authentic human welfare.

Much in fact depends on the underlying system of morality. On this subject the Church's social doctrine can make a specific contribution, since it is based on man's creation "in the image of God" (*Gen* 1:27), a datum which gives rise to the inviolable dignity of the human person and the transcendent value of natural moral norms. When business ethics prescinds from these two pillars, it inevitably risks losing its distinctive nature, and it falls prey to forms of exploitation; more specifically, it risks becoming subservient to existing economic and financial systems rather than correcting their dysfunctional aspects. Among other things, it risks being used to justify the financing of projects that are in reality unethical. The word "ethical", then, should not be used to make ideological distinctions, as if to suggest that initiatives not formally so designated would not be ethical. Efforts are needed—and it is essential to say this—not only to create "ethical" sectors or segments of the economy or the world of finance, but to ensure that the whole economy—the whole of finance—is ethical, not merely by virtue of an external label, but by its respect for requirements intrinsic to its very nature. The Church's social teaching is quite clear on the subject, recalling that the economy, in all its branches, constitutes a sector of human activity.[113]

46. When we consider the issues involved in the *relationship between business and ethics*, as well as the evolution currently taking place in methods of production, it would appear that the traditionally valid distinction between profit-based companies and non-profit organizations can no longer do full justice to reality or offer practical direction for the future. In recent decades a broad intermediate area has emerged

---

[113] Cf. Paul VI, Encyclical Letter *Populorum Progressio*, 14: *loc. cit.*, 264; John Paul II, Encyclical Letter *Centesimus Annus*, 32: *loc. cit.*, 832–833.

between the two types of enterprise. It is made up of traditional companies which nonetheless subscribe to social aid agreements in support of underdeveloped countries, charitable foundations associated with individual companies, groups of companies oriented towards social welfare, and the diversified world of the so-called "civil economy" and the "economy of communion". This is a matter not merely of a "third sector", but of a broad new composite reality embracing the private and public spheres, one which does not exclude profit but instead considers it a means for achieving human and social ends. Whether such companies distribute dividends or not, whether their juridical structure corresponds to one or other of the established forms, becomes secondary in relation to their willingness to view profit as a means of achieving the goal of a more humane market and society. It is to be hoped that these new kinds of enterprise will succeed in finding a suitable juridical and fiscal structure in every country. Without prejudice to the importance and the economic and social benefits of the more traditional forms of business, they steer the system towards a clearer and more complete assumption of duties on the part of economic subjects. And not only that. *The very plurality of institutional forms of business gives rise to a market which is not only more civilized but also more competitive.*

47. The strengthening of different types of businesses, especially those capable of viewing profit as a means for achieving the goal of a more humane market and society, must also be pursued in those countries that are excluded or marginalized from the influential circles of the global economy. In these countries it is very important to move ahead with projects based on subsidiarity, suitably planned and managed, aimed at affirming rights yet also providing for the assumption of corresponding responsibilities. In *development programs*, the principle of the *centrality of the human person*, as the subject primarily responsible for development, must be preserved. The principal concern must be to improve the actual living conditions of the people in a given region, thus enabling them to carry out those duties which their poverty does not presently allow them to fulfill. Social concern must never be an abstract attitude. Development programs, if they are to be adapted to individual situations, need to be flexible; and the people who benefit from them ought to be directly involved in their planning and implementation. The criteria to be applied should aspire towards incremental development in a

context of solidarity—with careful monitoring of results—inasmuch as there are no universally valid solutions. Much depends on the way programs are managed in practice. "The peoples themselves have the prime responsibility to work for their own development. But they will not bring this about in isolation." [114] These words of Paul VI are all the more timely nowadays, as our world becomes progressively more integrated. The dynamics of inclusion are hardly automatic. Solutions need to be carefully designed to correspond to people's concrete lives, based on a prudential evaluation of each situation. Alongside macro-projects, there is a place for micro-projects, and above all there is need for the active mobilization of all the subjects of civil society, both juridical and physical persons.

International cooperation requires people who can be part of the process of economic and human development through the solidarity of their presence, supervision, training, and respect. From this standpoint, international organizations might question the actual effectiveness of their bureaucratic and administrative machinery, which is often excessively costly. At times it happens that

---

[114] Paul VI, Encyclical Letter *Populorum Progressio*, 77: *loc. cit.*, 295.

those who receive aid become subordinate to the aid-givers, and the poor serve to perpetuate expensive bureaucracies which consume an excessively high percentage of funds intended for development. Hence it is to be hoped that all international agencies and non-governmental organizations will commit themselves to complete transparency, informing donors and the public of the percentage of their income allocated to programs of cooperation, the actual content of those programs, and, finally, the detailed expenditure of the institution itself.

48. Today the subject of development is also closely related to the duties arising from *our relationship to the natural environment*. The environment is God's gift to everyone, and in our use of it we have a responsibility towards the poor, towards future generations, and towards humanity as a whole. When nature, including the human being, is viewed as the result of mere chance or evolutionary determinism, our sense of responsibility wanes. In nature, the believer recognizes the wonderful result of God's creative activity, which we may use responsibly to satisfy our legitimate needs, material or otherwise, while respecting the intrinsic balance of creation. If this vision is lost, we end up either considering nature an

untouchable taboo or, on the contrary, abusing it. Neither attitude is consonant with the Christian vision of nature as the fruit of God's creation.

Nature expresses a design of love and truth. It is prior to us, and it has been given to us by God as the setting for our life. Nature speaks to us of the Creator (cf. *Rom* 1:20) and his love for humanity. It is destined to be "recapitulated" in Christ at the end of time (cf. *Eph* 1:9–10; *Col* 1:19–20). Thus it too is a "vocation".[115] Nature is at our disposal, not as "a heap of scattered refuse",[116] but as a gift of the Creator, who has given it an inbuilt order, enabling man to draw from it the principles needed in order "to till it and keep it" (*Gen* 2:15). But it should also be stressed that it is contrary to authentic development to view nature as something more important than the human person. This position leads to attitudes of neo-paganism or a new pantheism—human salvation cannot come from nature alone, understood in a purely naturalistic sense. This having been said, it is also

---

[115] John Paul II, *Message for the 1990 World Day of Peace*, 6: *AAS* 82 (1990), 150.

[116] Heraclitus of Ephesus (Ephesus, ca. 535 B.C.–ca. 475 B.C.), Fragment 22B124, in H. Diels and W. Kranz, *Die Fragmente der Vorsokratiker*, Weidmann, Berlin, 1952, 6th ed.

necessary to reject the opposite position, which aims at total technical dominion over nature, because the natural environment is more than raw material to be manipulated at our pleasure; it is a wondrous work of the Creator containing a "grammar" which sets forth ends and criteria for its wise use, not its reckless exploitation. Today much harm is done to development precisely as a result of these distorted notions. Reducing nature merely to a collection of contingent data ends up doing violence to the environment and even encouraging activity that fails to respect human nature itself. Our nature, constituted not only by matter but also by spirit and, as such, endowed with transcendent meaning and aspirations, is also normative for culture. Human beings interpret and shape the natural environment through culture, which in turn is given direction by the responsible use of freedom, in accordance with the dictates of the moral law. Consequently, projects for integral human development cannot ignore coming generations but need to be marked by solidarity and *intergenerational justice*, while taking into account a variety of contexts: ecological, juridical, economic, political, and cultural.[117]

---

[117] Pontifical Council for Justice and Peace, *Compendium of the Social Doctrine of the Church*, 451–487.

49. Questions linked to the care and preservation of the environment today need to give due consideration to *the energy problem*. The fact that some States, power groups, and companies hoard non-renewable energy resources represents a grave obstacle to development in poor countries. Those countries lack the economic means either to gain access to existing sources of non-renewable energy or to finance research into new alternatives. The stockpiling of natural resources, which in many cases are found in the poor countries themselves, gives rise to exploitation and frequent conflicts between and within nations. These conflicts are often fought on the soil of those same countries, with a heavy toll of death, destruction, and further decay. The international community has an urgent duty to find institutional means of regulating the exploitation of non-renewable resources, involving poor countries in the process, in order to plan together for the future.

On this front too, there is a *pressing moral need for renewed solidarity*, especially in relationships between developing countries and those that are highly industrialized.[118] The technologically

---

[118] Cf. John Paul II, *Message for the 1990 World Day of Peace*, 10: *loc. cit.*, 152–153.

advanced societies can and must lower their
domestic energy consumption, either through
an evolution in manufacturing methods or
through greater ecological sensitivity among their
citizens. It should be added that at present it is
possible to achieve improved energy efficiency
while at the same time encouraging research into
alternative forms of energy. What is also needed,
though, is a worldwide redistribution of energy
resources, so that countries lacking those
resources can have access to them. The fate of
those countries cannot be left in the hands of
whoever is first to claim the spoils or whoever
is able to prevail over the rest. Here we are dealing with major issues; if they are to be faced adequately, then everyone must responsibly
recognize the impact they will have on future
generations, particularly on the many young people in the poorer nations, who "ask to assume
their active part in the construction of a better
world".[119]

50. This responsibility is a global one, for it is
concerned not just with energy but with the
whole of creation, which must not be
bequeathed to future generations depleted of its
resources. Human beings legitimately exercise a

---

[119] Paul VI, Encyclical Letter *Populorum Progressio*, 65: *loc. cit.*, 289.

responsible stewardship over nature, in order to protect it, to enjoy its fruits, and to cultivate it in new ways, with the assistance of advanced technologies, so that it can worthily accommodate and feed the world's population. On this earth there is room for everyone: here the entire human family must find the resources to live with dignity, through the help of nature itself—God's gift to his children—and through hard work and creativity. At the same time we must recognize our grave duty to hand the earth on to future generations in such a condition that they too can worthily inhabit it and continue to cultivate it. This means being committed to making joint decisions "after pondering responsibly the road to be taken, decisions aimed at strengthening that *covenant between human beings and the environment* which should mirror the creative love of God, from whom we come and towards whom we are journeying".[120] Let us hope that the international community and individual governments will succeed in countering harmful ways of treating the environment. It is likewise incumbent upon the competent authorities to make every effort to ensure that the economic and social costs of using up shared

---

[120] Benedict XVI, *Message for the 2008 World Day of Peace*, 7: *AAS* 100 (2008), 41.

environmental resources are recognized with
transparency and fully borne by those who incur
them, not by other peoples or future generations: the protection of the environment, of
resources, and of the climate obliges all international leaders to act jointly and to show a readi-
ness to work in good faith, respecting the law
and promoting solidarity with the weakest
regions of the planet.[121] One of the greatest challenges facing the economy is to achieve the most
efficient use—not abuse—of natural resources,
based on a realization that the notion of "efficiency" is not value-free.

51. *The way humanity treats the environment influences the way it treats itself, and vice versa.* This invites
contemporary society to a serious review of its
lifestyle, which, in many parts of the world, is
prone to hedonism and consumerism, regard-
less of their harmful consequences.[122] What is
needed is an effective shift in mentality which
can lead to the adoption of *new lifestyles* "in
which the quest for truth, beauty, goodness,
and communion with others for the sake of

---

[121] Cf. Benedict XVI, *Address to the General Assembly of the United
Nations Organization*, New York, 18 April 2008.
[122] Cf. John Paul II, *Message for the 1990 World Day of Peace*, 13:
loc. cit., 154–155.

common growth are the factors which determine consumer choices, savings, and investments." [123] Every violation of solidarity and civic friendship harms the environment, just as environmental deterioration in turn upsets relations in society. Nature, especially in our time, is so integrated into the dynamics of society and culture that by now it hardly constitutes an independent variable. Desertification and the decline in productivity in some agricultural areas are also the result of impoverishment and underdevelopment among their inhabitants. When incentives are offered for their economic and cultural development, nature itself is protected. Moreover, how many natural resources are squandered by wars! Peace in and among peoples would also provide greater protection for nature. The hoarding of resources, especially water, can generate serious conflicts among the peoples involved. Peaceful agreement about the use of resources can protect nature and, at the same time, the well-being of the societies concerned.

The Church has a responsibility towards creation, and she must assert this responsibility in the

---

[123] John Paul II, Encyclical Letter *Centesimus Annus*, 36: *loc. cit.*, 838–840.

public sphere. In so doing, she must defend not only earth, water, and air as gifts of creation that belong to everyone. She must above all protect mankind from self-destruction. There is need for what might be called a human ecology, correctly understood. The deterioration of nature is in fact closely connected to the culture that shapes human coexistence: *when "human ecology"*[124] *is respected within society, environmental ecology also benefits.* Just as human virtues are interrelated, such that the weakening of one places others at risk, so the ecological system is based on respect for a plan that affects both the health of society and its good relationship with nature.

In order to protect nature, it is not enough to intervene with economic incentives or deterrents; not even an apposite education is sufficient. These are important steps, but *the decisive issue is the overall moral tenor of society.* If there is a lack of respect for the right to life and to a natural death, if human conception, gestation, and birth are made artificial, if human embryos are sacrificed to research, the conscience of society ends up losing the

---

[124] *Ibid.*, 38: *loc. cit.*, 840–841; Benedict XVI, *Message for the 2007 World Day of Peace*, 8: *loc. cit.*, 779.

concept of human ecology and, along with
it, that of environmental ecology. It is con-
tradictory to insist that future generations
respect the natural environment when our educational systems and laws do not help them
to respect themselves. The book of nature is
one and indivisible: it takes in not only the
environment but also life, sexuality, marriage,
the family, social relations: in a word, integral
human development. Our duties towards the
environment are linked to our duties towards
the human person, considered in himself and
in relation to others. It would be wrong to
uphold one set of duties while trampling on
the other. Herein lies a grave contradiction
in our mentality and practice today: one which
demeans the person, disrupts the environment, and damages society.

52. Truth and the love which it reveals cannot
be produced: they can only be received as a
gift. Their ultimate source is not, and cannot
be, mankind, but only God, who is himself
Truth and Love. This principle is extremely
important for society and for development, since
neither can be a purely human product; the
vocation to development on the part of individuals and peoples is not based simply on
human choice but is an intrinsic part of a plan

that is prior to us and constitutes for all of us a duty to be freely accepted. That which is prior to us and constitutes us—subsistent Love and Truth—shows us what goodness is and in what our true happiness consists. *It shows us the road to true development.*

CHAPTER FIVE

The Cooperation of the
Human Family

53. One of the deepest forms of poverty a person can experience is isolation. If we look closely at other kinds of poverty, including material forms, we see that they are born from isolation, from not being loved, or from difficulties in being able to love. Poverty is often produced by a rejection of God's love, by man's basic and tragic tendency to close in on himself, thinking himself to be self-sufficient or merely an insignificant and ephemeral fact, a "stranger" in a random universe. Man is alienated when he is alone, when he is detached from reality, when he stops thinking and believing in a foundation.[125] All of humanity is alienated when too much trust is placed in merely human projects, ideologies, and false utopias.[126] Today humanity appears much more interactive than in the past: this shared sense of being close to one another must be transformed

---

[125] Cf. John Paul II, Encyclical Letter *Centesimus Annus*, 41: *loc. cit.*, 843–845.
[126] Cf. *ibid.*

into true communion. *The development of peoples depends, above all, on a recognition that the human race is a single family* working together in true communion, not simply a group of subjects who happen to live side by side.[127]

Pope Paul VI noted that "the world is in trouble because of the lack of thinking."[128] He was making an observation but also expressing a wish: a new trajectory of thinking is needed in order to arrive at a better understanding of the implications of our being one family; interaction among the peoples of the world calls us to embark upon this new trajectory, so that integration can signify solidarity[129] rather than marginalization. Thinking of this kind requires a *deeper critical evaluation of the category of relation*. This is a task that cannot be undertaken by the social sciences alone, insofar as the contribution of disciplines such as metaphysics and theology is needed if man's transcendent dignity is to be properly understood.

---

[127] Cf. John Paul II, Encyclical Letter *Evangelium Vitae*, 20: *loc. cit.*, 422–424.

[128] Encyclical Letter *Populorum Progressio*, 85: *loc. cit.*, 298–299.

[129] Cf. John Paul II, *Message for the 1998 World Day of Peace*, 3: *AAS* 90 (1998), 150; *Address to the Members of the Vatican Foundation "Centesimus Annus—Pro Pontifice"*, 9 May 1998, 2; *Address to the Civil Authorities and Diplomatic Corps of Austria*, 20 June 1998, 8; *Message to the Catholic University of the Sacred Heart*, 5 May 2000, 6.

As a spiritual being, the human creature is defined through interpersonal relations. The more authentically he or she lives these relations, the more his or her own personal identity matures. It is not by isolation that man establishes his worth, but by placing himself in relation with others and with God. Hence these relations take on fundamental importance. The same holds true for peoples as well. A metaphysical understanding of the relations between persons is therefore of great benefit for their development. In this regard, reason finds inspiration and direction in Christian revelation, according to which the human community does not absorb the individual, annihilating his autonomy, as happens in the various forms of totalitarianism, but rather values him all the more because the relation between individual and community is a relation between one totality and another.[130] Just as a family does not submerge the identities of its individual members, just as the Church rejoices in each "new creation" (*Gal* 6:15; *2 Cor* 5:17) incorporated by Baptism into her living Body, so too the

---

[130] According to Saint Thomas, *"ratio partis contrariatur rationi personae"*, *In III Sent.*, d. 5, q. 3, a. 2; also *"Homo non ordinatur ad communitatem politicam secundum se totum et secundum omnia sua"*, *Summa Theologiae* I-II, q. 21, a. 4, ad 3.

unity of the human family does not submerge the identities of individuals, peoples, and cultures, but makes them more transparent to each other and links them more closely in their legitimate diversity.

54. The theme of development can be identified with the inclusion-in-relation of all individuals and peoples within the one community of the human family, built in solidarity on the basis of the fundamental values of justice and peace. This perspective is illuminated in a striking way by the relationship between the Persons of the Trinity within the one divine Substance. The Trinity is absolute unity insofar as the three divine Persons are pure relationality. The reciprocal transparency among the divine Persons is total, and the bond between each of them complete, since they constitute a unique and absolute unity. God desires to incorporate us into this reality of communion as well: "that they may be one even as we are one" (*Jn* 17:22). The Church is a sign and instrument of this unity.[131] Relationships between human beings throughout history cannot but be enriched by reference

---

[131] Cf. Second Vatican Ecumenical Council, Dogmatic Constitution on the Church *Lumen Gentium*, 1.

to this divine model. In particular, *in the light of the revealed mystery of the Trinity*, we understand that true openness means, not loss of individual identity, but profound interpenetration. This also emerges from the common human experiences of love and truth. Just as the sacramental love of spouses unites them spiritually in "one flesh" (*Gen* 2:24; *Mt* 19:5; *Eph* 5:31) and makes out of the two a real and relational unity, so in an analogous way truth unites spirits and causes them to think in unison, attracting them as a unity to itself.

55. The Christian revelation of the unity of the human race presupposes a *metaphysical interpretation of the "humanum" in which relationality is an essential element*. Other cultures and religions teach brotherhood and peace and are therefore of enormous importance to integral human development. Some religious and cultural attitudes, however, do not fully embrace the principle of love and truth and therefore end up retarding or even obstructing authentic human development. There are certain religious cultures in the world today that do not oblige men and women to live in communion but rather cut them off from one another in a search for individual well-being, limited

to the gratification of psychological desires. Furthermore, a certain proliferation of different religious "paths", attracting small groups or even single individuals, together with religious syncretism, can give rise to separation and disengagement. One possible negative effect of the process of globalization is the tendency to favor this kind of syncretism[132] by encouraging forms of "religion" that, instead of bringing people together, alienate them from one another and distance them from reality. At the same time, some religious and cultural traditions persist which ossify society in rigid social groupings, in magical beliefs that fail to respect the dignity of the person, and in attitudes of subjugation to occult powers. In these contexts, love and truth have difficulty asserting themselves, and authentic development is impeded.

For this reason, while it may be true that development needs the religions and cultures of different peoples, it is equally true that adequate discernment is needed. Religious freedom does not mean religious indifferentism,

---

[132] Cf. John Paul II, *Address to the Sixth Public Session of the Pontifical Academies of Theology and of Saint Thomas Aquinas,* 8 November 2001, 3.

nor does it imply that all religions are equal.[133] Discernment is needed regarding the contribution of cultures and religions, especially on the part of those who wield political power, if the social community is to be built up in a spirit of respect for the common good. Such discernment has to be based on the criterion of charity and truth. Since the development of persons and peoples is at stake, this discernment will have to take account of the need for emancipation and inclusivity, in the context of a truly universal human community. "The whole man and all men" is also the criterion for evaluating cultures and religions. Christianity, the religion of the "God who has a human face",[134] contains this very criterion within itself.

56. The Christian religion and other religions can offer their contribution to development *only if God has a place in the public realm*, specifically

---

[133] Cf. Congregation for the Doctrine of the Faith, Declaration on the Unicity and Salvific Universality of Jesus Christ and the Church *Dominus Iesus* (6 August 2000), 22: *AAS* 92 (2000), 763–764; *idem, Doctrinal Note on Some Questions Regarding the Participation of Catholics in Political Life* (24 November 2002), 8: *AAS* 96 (2004), 369–370.

[134] Benedict XVI, Encyclical Letter *Spe Salvi*, 31: *loc. cit.*, 1010; *Address to the Participants in the Fourth National Congress of the Church in Italy*, Verona, 19 October 2006.

in regard to its cultural, social, economic, and particularly its political dimensions. The Church's social doctrine came into being in order to claim "citizenship status" for the Christian religion.[135] Denying the right to profess one's religion in public and the right to bring the truths of faith to bear upon public life has negative consequences for true development. The exclusion of religion from the public square—and, at the other extreme, religious fundamentalism—hinders an encounter between persons and their collaboration for the progress of humanity. Public life is sapped of its motivation, and politics takes on a domineering and aggressive character. Human rights risk being ignored either because they are robbed of their transcendent foundation or because personal freedom is not acknowledged. Secularism and fundamentalism exclude the possibility of fruitful dialogue and effective cooperation between reason and religious faith. *Reason always stands in need of being purified by faith*: this also holds true for political reason, which must not consider itself omnipotent. For its part, *religion always needs to be purified by reason* in order to show its authentically human face. Any breach

---

[135] John Paul II, Encyclical Letter *Centesimus Annus*, 5: *loc. cit.*, 798–800; Benedict XVI, *Address to the Participants in the Fourth National Congress of the Church in Italy*, Verona, 19 October 2006.

in this dialogue comes only at an enormous price to human development.

57. Fruitful dialogue between faith and reason cannot but render the work of charity more effective within society, and it constitutes the most appropriate framework for promoting *fraternal collaboration between believers and non-believers* in their shared commitment to working for justice and the peace of the human family. In the Pastoral Constitution *Gaudium et Spes*, the Council fathers asserted that "believers and unbelievers agree almost unanimously that all things on earth should be ordered towards man as to their center and summit." [136] For believers, the world derives neither from blind chance nor from strict necessity, but from God's plan. This is what gives rise to the duty of believers to unite their efforts with those of all men and women of good will, with the followers of other religions and with non-believers, so that this world of ours may effectively correspond to the divine plan: living as a family under the Creator's watchful eye. A particular manifestation of charity and a guiding criterion for fraternal cooperation between believers and non-believers is undoubtedly the *principle of*

---

[136] No. 12.

subsidiarity,[137] an expression of inalienable human freedom. Subsidiarity is first and foremost a form of assistance to the human person via the autonomy of intermediate bodies. Such assistance is offered when individuals or groups are unable to accomplish something on their own, and it is always designed to achieve their emancipation, because it fosters freedom and participation through assumption of responsibility. Subsidiarity respects personal dignity by recognizing in the person a subject who is always capable of giving something to others. By considering reciprocity as the heart of what it is to be a human being, subsidiarity is the most effective antidote against any form of all-encompassing welfare state. It is able to take account both of the manifold articulation of plans—and therefore of the plurality of subjects—as well as the coordination of those plans. Hence the principle of subsidiarity is particularly well-suited to managing globalization and directing it towards authentic human development. In order not to produce a dangerous universal power of a tyrannical nature, *the governance of globalization*

---

[137] Cf. Pius XI, Encyclical Letter *Quadragesimo Anno* (15 May 1931): *AAS* 23 (1931), 203; John Paul II, Encyclical Letter *Centesimus Annus*, 48: *loc. cit.*, 852–854; *Catechism of the Catholic Church*, 1883.

must be marked by subsidiarity, articulated into several layers and involving different levels that can work together. Globalization certainly requires authority, insofar as it poses the problem of a global common good that needs to be pursued. This authority, however, must be organized in a subsidiary and stratified way[138] if it is not to infringe upon freedom and if it is to yield effective results in practice.

58. *The principle of subsidiarity must remain closely linked to the principle of solidarity and vice versa,* since the former without the latter gives way to social privatism, while the latter without the former gives way to paternalist social assistance that is demeaning to those in need. This general rule must also be taken broadly into consideration when addressing issues concerning *international development aid.* Such aid, whatever the donors' intentions, can sometimes lock people into a state of dependence and even foster situations of localized oppression and exploitation in the receiving country. Economic aid, in order to be true to its purpose, must not pursue secondary objectives. It must be distributed with the involvement of not only the governments of receiving countries, but also

---

[138] Cf. John XXIII, Encyclical Letter *Pacem in Terris, loc. cit.,* 274.

local economic agents and the bearers of culture within civil society, including local Churches. Aid programs must increasingly acquire the characteristics of participation and completion from the grass roots. Indeed, the most valuable resources in countries receiving development aid are human resources: herein lies the real capital that needs to accumulate in order to guarantee a truly autonomous future for the poorest countries. It should also be remembered that, in the economic sphere, the principal form of assistance needed by developing countries is that of allowing and encouraging the gradual penetration of their products into international markets, thus making it possible for these countries to participate fully in international economic life. Too often in the past, aid has served to create only fringe markets for the products of these donor countries. This was often due to a lack of genuine demand for the products in question: it is therefore necessary to help such countries improve their products and adapt them more effectively to existing demand. Furthermore, there are those who fear the effects of competition through the importation of products—normally agricultural products—from economically poor countries. Nevertheless, it should be remembered that for such countries, the possibility of marketing their products is very often what guarantees their survival in both the short and long term. Just and equitable international trade in agricultural goods can be beneficial to everyone, both to suppliers and to customers. For this reason, not only is commercial orientation needed for production of this kind, but also the establishment of international trade regulations to support it and stronger financing for development in order to increase the productivity of these economies.

59. *Cooperation for development* must not be concerned exclusively with the economic dimension: it offers a wonderful *opportunity for encounter between cultures and peoples*. If the parties to cooperation on the side of economically developed countries—as occasionally happens—fail to take account of their own or others' cultural identity, or the human values that shape it, they cannot enter into meaningful dialogue with the citizens of poor countries. If the latter, in their turn, are uncritically and indiscriminately open to every cultural proposal, they will not be in a position to assume responsibility for their own authentic development.[139] Technologically

---

[139] Cf. Paul VI, Encyclical Letter *Populorum Progressio*, 10, 41: *loc. cit.*, 262, 277–278.

advanced societies must not confuse their own technological development with a presumed cultural superiority, but they must rather rediscover within themselves the oft-forgotten virtues which made it possible for them to flourish throughout their history. Evolving societies must remain faithful to all that is truly human in their traditions, avoiding the temptation to overlay them automatically with the mechanisms of a globalized technological civilization. In all cultures there are examples of ethical convergence, some isolated, some interrelated, as an expression of the one human nature, willed by the Creator; the tradition of ethical wisdom knows this as the natural law.[140] This universal moral law provides a sound basis for all cultural, religious, and political dialogue, and it ensures that the multifaceted pluralism of cultural diversity does not detach itself from the common quest for truth, goodness, and God. Thus adherence to the law etched on human hearts is the precondition for all constructive social cooperation. Every culture has burdens from which it must be freed and shadows from which it must emerge. The Christian faith, by

---

[140] Cf. Benedict XVI, *Address to Members of the International Theological Commission*, 5 October 2007; *Address to the Participants in the International Congress on Natural Moral Law*, 12 February 2007.

becoming incarnate in cultures and at the same time transcending them, can help them grow in universal brotherhood and solidarity, for the advancement of global and community development.

60. In the search for solutions to the current economic crisis, *development aid for poor countries must be considered a valid means of creating wealth for all.* What aid program is there that can hold out such significant growth prospects—even from the point of view of the world economy—as the support of populations that are still in the initial or early phases of economic development? From this perspective, more economically developed nations should do all they can to allocate larger portions of their gross domestic product to development aid, thus respecting the obligations that the international community has undertaken in this regard. One way of doing so is by reviewing their internal social assistance and welfare policies, applying the principle of subsidiarity, and creating better integrated welfare systems, with the active participation of private individuals and civil society. In this way, it is actually possible to improve social services and welfare programs and at the same time to save resources—by eliminating waste and rejecting fraudulent claims—which could then be allocated to international

solidarity. A more devolved and organic system of social solidarity, less bureaucratic but no less coordinated, would make it possible to harness much dormant energy for the benefit of solidarity between peoples.

One possible approach to development aid would be to apply effectively what is known as fiscal subsidiarity, allowing citizens to decide how to allocate a portion of the taxes they pay to the State. Provided it does not degenerate into the promotion of special interests, this can help to stimulate forms of welfare solidarity from below, with obvious benefits in the area of solidarity for development as well.

61. Greater solidarity at the international level is seen especially in the ongoing promotion— even in the midst of economic crisis—of *greater access to education*, which is at the same time an essential precondition for effective international cooperation. The term "education" refers not only to classroom teaching and vocational training—both of which are important factors in development—but to the complete formation of the person. In this regard, there is a problem that should be highlighted: in order to educate, it is necessary to know the nature of the human person, to know who he or she is. The

increasing prominence of a relativistic understanding of that nature presents serious problems for education, especially moral education,
jeopardizing its universal extension. Yielding to
this kind of relativism makes everyone poorer and
has a negative impact on the effectiveness of aid
to the most needy populations, who lack not
only economic and technical means, but also
educational methods and resources to assist people in realizing their full human potential.

An illustration of the significance of this problem is offered by the phenomenon of *international
tourism*,[141] which can be a major factor in economic development and cultural growth, but can
also become an occasion for exploitation and
moral degradation. The current situation offers
unique opportunities for the economic aspects
of development—that is to say, the flow of money
and the emergence of a significant amount of
local enterprise—to be combined with the cultural aspects, chief among which is education.
In many cases this is what happens, but in other
cases international tourism has a negative educational impact both for the tourist and the local
populace. The latter are often exposed to

---

[141] Cf. Benedict XVI, *Address to the Bishops of Thailand on Their
"Ad Limina" Visit*, 16 May 2008.

immoral or even perverted forms of conduct, as in the case of so-called sex tourism, to which many human beings are sacrificed even at a tender age. It is sad to note that this activity often takes place with the support of local governments, with silence from those in the tourists' countries of origin, and with the complicity of many of the tour operators. Even in less extreme cases, international tourism often follows a consumerist and hedonistic pattern, as a form of escapism planned in a manner typical of the countries of origin and, therefore, not conducive to authentic encounter between persons and cultures. We need, therefore, to develop a different type of tourism that has the ability to promote genuine mutual understanding, without taking away from the element of rest and healthy recreation. Tourism of this type needs to increase, partly through closer coordination with the experience gained from international cooperation and enterprise for development.

62. Another aspect of integral human development that is worthy of attention is the phenomenon of *migration*. This is a striking phenomenon because of the sheer numbers of people involved, the social, economic, political, cultural, and religious problems it raises,

and the dramatic challenges it poses to nations and the international community. We can say that we are facing a social phenomenon of epoch-making proportions that requires bold, forward-looking policies of international coop-eration if it is to be handled effectively. Such policies should set out from close collabo-ration between the migrants' countries of ori-gin and their countries of destination; it should be accompanied by adequate international norms able to coordinate different legislative systems with a view to safeguarding the needs and rights of individual migrants and their fam-ilies and, at the same time, those of the host countries. No country can be expected to address today's problems of migration by itself. We are all witnesses of the burden of suffer-ing, the dislocation, and the aspirations that accompany the flow of migrants. The phe-nomenon, as everyone knows, is difficult to manage; but there is no doubt that foreign workers, despite any difficulties concerning integration, make a significant contribution to the economic development of the host coun-try through their labor, besides that which they make to their country of origin through the money they send home. Obviously, these labor-ers cannot be considered as a commodity or a mere workforce. They must not, therefore, be treated like any other factor of production. Every migrant is a human person who, as such, possesses fundamental, inalienable rights that must be respected by everyone and in every circumstance.[142]

63. No consideration of the problems associated with development could fail to highlight the direct link between *poverty and unemployment*. In many cases, poverty results from a *violation of the dignity of human work*, either because work opportunities are limited (through unemployment or underemployment) or "because a low value is put on work and the rights that flow from it, especially the right to a just wage and to the personal security of the worker and his or her family".[143] For this reason, on 1 May 2000, on the occasion of the Jubilee of Workers, my venerable predecessor Pope John Paul II issued an appeal for "a global coalition in favor of 'decent work'",[144] supporting the strategy of the International Labour Organization. In this way, he

---

[142] Cf. Pontifical Council for the Pastoral Care of Migrants and Itinerant People, Instruction *Erga Migrantes Caritas Christi* (3 May 2004): *AAS* 96 (2004), 762–822.

[143] John Paul II, Encyclical Letter *Laborem Exercens*, 8: *loc. cit.*, 594–598.

[144] Jubilee of Workers, *Greeting after Mass*, 1 May 2000.

gave a strong moral impetus to this objective, seeing it as an aspiration of families in every country of the world. What is meant by the word "decency" in regard to work? It means work that expresses the essential dignity of every man and woman in the context of their particular society: work that is freely chosen, effectively associating workers, both men and women, with the development of their community; work that enables the worker to be respected and free from any form of discrimination; work that makes it possible for families to meet their needs and provide schooling for their children, without the children themselves being forced into labor; work that permits the workers to organize themselves freely and to make their voices heard; work that leaves enough room for rediscovering one's roots at a personal, familial, and spiritual level; work that guarantees those who have retired a decent standard of living.

64. While reflecting on the theme of work, it is appropriate to recall how important it is that *labor unions*—which have always been encouraged and supported by the Church—should be open to the new perspectives that are emerging in the world of work. Looking to wider concerns than the specific category of labor for which they were

formed, union organizations are called to address some of the new questions arising in our society: I am thinking, for example, of the complex of issues that social scientists describe in terms of a conflict between worker and consumer. Without necessarily endorsing the thesis that the central focus on the worker has given way to a central focus on the consumer, this would still appear to constitute new ground for unions to explore creatively. The global context in which work takes place also demands that national labor unions, which tend to limit themselves to defending the interests of their registered members, should turn their attention to those outside their membership and, in particular, to workers in developing countries where social rights are often violated. The protection of these workers, partly achieved through appropriate initiatives aimed at their countries of origin, will enable trade unions to demonstrate the authentic ethical and cultural motivations that made it possible for them, in a different social and labor context, to play a decisive role in development. The Church's traditional teaching makes a valid distinction between the respective roles and functions of trade unions and politics. This distinction allows unions to identify civil society as the proper setting for their necessary activity of defending and promoting labor, especially on behalf of exploited and unrepresented workers, whose woeful condition is often ignored by the distracted eye of society.

65. *Finance*, therefore—through the renewed structures and operating methods that have to be designed after its misuse, which wreaked such havoc on the real economy—now needs to go back to being an *instrument directed towards improved wealth creation and development*. Insofar as they are instruments, the entire economy and finance, not just certain sectors, must be used in an ethical way so as to create suitable conditions for human development and for the development of peoples. It is certainly useful, and in some circumstances imperative, to launch financial initiatives in which the humanitarian dimension predominates. However, this must not obscure the fact that the entire financial system has to be aimed at sustaining true development. Above all, the intention to do good must not be considered incompatible with the effective capacity to produce goods. Financiers must rediscover the genuinely ethical foundation of their activity so as not to abuse the sophisticated instruments which can serve to betray the interests of savers. Right intention, transparency, and the search for positive results are mutually compatible and must never be

detached from one another. If love is wise, it can find ways of working in accordance with provident and just expediency, as is illustrated in a significant way by much of the experience of credit unions.

Both the regulation of the financial sector, so as to safeguard weaker parties and discourage scandalous speculation, and experimentation with new forms of finance, designed to support development projects, are positive experiences that should be further explored and encouraged, highlighting *the responsibility of the investor*. Furthermore, the *experience of microfinance*, which has its roots in the thinking and activity of the civil humanists—I am thinking especially of the birth of pawnbroking—should be strengthened and fine-tuned. This is all the more necessary in these days when financial difficulties can become severe for many of the more vulnerable sectors of the population, who should be protected from the risk of usury and from despair. The weakest members of society should be helped to defend themselves against usury, just as poor peoples should be helped to derive real benefit from micro-credit, in order to discourage the exploitation that is possible in these two areas. Since rich countries are also experiencing new forms of poverty, micro-finance can give practical assistance by launching new initiatives and opening up new sectors for the benefit of the weaker elements in society, even at a time of general economic downturn.

66. Global interconnectedness has led to the emergence of a new political power, that of *consumers and their associations*. This is a phenomenon that needs to be further explored, as it contains positive elements to be encouraged as well as excesses to be avoided. It is good for people to realize that purchasing is always a moral—and not simply economic— act. Hence *the consumer has a specific social responsibility*, which goes hand in hand with the social responsibility of the enterprise. Consumers should be continually educated[145] regarding their daily role, which can be exercised with respect for moral principles without diminishing the intrinsic economic rationality of the act of purchasing. In the retail industry, particularly at times like the present, when purchasing power has diminished and people must live more frugally, it is necessary to explore other paths: for example, forms of

---

[145] Cf. John Paul II, Encyclical Letter *Centesimus Annus*, 36: *loc. cit.*, 838–840.

cooperative purchasing like the consumer cooperatives that have been in operation since the nineteenth century, partly through the initiative of Catholics. In addition, it can be helpful to promote new ways of marketing products from deprived areas of the world, so as to guarantee their producers a decent return. However, certain conditions need to be met: the market should be genuinely transparent; the producers, as well as increasing their profit margins, should also receive improved formation in professional skills and technology; and finally, trade of this kind must not become hostage to partisan ideologies. A more incisive role for consumers, as long as they themselves are not manipulated by associations that do not truly represent them, is a desirable element for building economic democracy.

67. In the face of the unrelenting growth of global interdependence, there is a strongly felt need, even in the midst of a global recession, for a reform of the *United Nations Organization* and, likewise, of *economic institutions and international finance,* so that the concept of the family of nations can acquire real teeth. One also senses the urgent need to find innovative ways of implementing the principle of the

responsibility to protect[146] and of giving poorer nations an effective voice in shared decision-making. This seems necessary in order to arrive at a political, juridical, and economic order which can increase and give direction to international cooperation for the development of all peoples in solidarity. To manage the global economy; to revive economies hit by the crisis; to avoid any deterioration of the present crisis and the greater imbalances that would result; to bring about integral and timely disarmament, food security, and peace; to guarantee the protection of the environment and to regulate migration: for all this, there is urgent need of a true *world political authority*, as my predecessor Blessed John XXIII indicated some years ago. Such an authority would need to be regulated by law, to observe consistently the principles of subsidiarity and solidarity, to seek to establish the common good,[147] and *to make a commitment to securing authentic integral human development inspired by the values of charity in truth*. Furthermore, such an authority would need to be universally recognized and

---

[146] Cf. Benedict XVI, *Address to the Members of the General Assembly of the United Nations Organization*, New York, 18 April 2008.

[147] Cf. John XXIII, Encyclical Letter *Pacem in Terris, loc. cit.*, 293; Pontifical Council for Justice and Peace, *Compendium of the Social Doctrine of the Church*, 441.

to be vested with the effective power to ensure security for all, regard for justice, and respect for rights.[148] Obviously it would have to have the authority to ensure compliance with its decisions from all parties and also with the coordinated measures adopted in various international forums. Without this, despite the great progress accomplished in various sectors, international law would risk being conditioned by the balance of power among the strongest nations. The integral development of peoples and international cooperation require the establishment of a greater degree of international ordering, marked by subsidiarity, for the management of globalization.[149] They also require the construction of a social order that at last conforms to the moral order, to the interconnection between moral and social spheres, and to the link between politics and the economic and civil spheres, as envisaged by the Charter of the United Nations.

---

[148] Cf. Second Vatican Ecumenical Council, Pastoral Constitution on the Church in the Modern World *Gaudium et Spes*, 82.

[149] Cf. John Paul II, Encyclical Letter *Sollicitudo Rei Socialis*, 43: *loc. cit.*, 574–575.

CHAPTER SIX

The Development of Peoples and Technology

68. The development of peoples is intimately linked to the development of individuals. The human person by nature is actively involved in his own development. The development in question is not simply the result of natural mechanisms, since, as everybody knows, we are all capable of making free and responsible choices. Nor is it merely at the mercy of our caprice, since we all know that we are a gift, not something self-generated. Our freedom is profoundly shaped by our being and by its limits. No one shapes his own conscience arbitrarily, but we all build our own "I" on the basis of a "self" which is given to us. Not only are other persons outside our control, but each one of us is outside his or her own control. *A person's development is compromised if he claims to be solely responsible for producing what he becomes.* By analogy, the development of peoples goes awry if humanity thinks it can recreate itself through the "wonders" of technology, just as economic development is

exposed as a destructive sham if it relies on the "wonders" of finance in order to sustain unnatural and consumerist growth. In the face of such Promethean presumption, we must fortify our love for a freedom that is not merely arbitrary, but is rendered truly human by acknowledgment of the good that underlies it. To this end, man needs to look inside himself in order to recognize the fundamental norms of the natural moral law which God has written on our hearts.

69. The challenge of development today is closely linked to *technological progress*, with its astounding applications in the field of biology. Technology—it is worth emphasizing—is a profoundly human reality, linked to the autonomy and freedom of man. In technology we express and confirm the hegemony of the spirit over matter. "The human spirit, 'increasingly free of its bondage to creatures, can be more easily drawn to the worship and contemplation of the Creator'." [150] Technology enables us to exercise dominion over matter, to reduce risks, to save labor, to improve our conditions of life. It

---

[150] Paul VI, Encyclical Letter *Populorum Progressio*, 41: *loc. cit.*, 277–278; cf. Second Vatican Ecumenical Council, Pastoral Constitution on the Church in the Modern World *Gaudium et Spes*, 57.

touches the heart of the vocation of human labor: in technology, seen as the product of his genius, man recognizes himself and forges his own humanity. Technology is the objective side of human action,[151] whose origin and *raison d'être* are found in the subjective element: the worker himself. For this reason, technology is never merely technology. It reveals man and his aspirations towards development; it expresses the inner tension that impels him gradually to overcome material limitations. *Technology, in this sense, is a response to God's command to till and to keep the land* (cf. *Gen* 2:15) that he has entrusted to humanity, and it must serve to reinforce the covenant between human beings and the environment, a covenant that should mirror God's creative love.

70. Technological development can give rise to the idea that technology is self-sufficient when too much attention is given to the "*how*" questions and not enough to the many "*why*" questions underlying human activity. For this reason technology can appear ambivalent. Produced through human creativity as a tool of personal freedom, technology can be understood as

---

[151] Cf. John Paul II, Encyclical Letter *Laborem Exercens*, 5: *loc. cit.*, 586–589.

a manifestation of absolute freedom, the freedom that seeks to prescind from the limits inherent in things. The process of globalization could replace ideologies with technology,[152] allowing the latter to become an ideological power that threatens to confine us within an *a priori* that holds us back from encountering being and truth. Were that to happen, we would all know, evaluate, and make decisions about our life situations from within a technocratic cultural perspective to which we would belong structurally, without ever being able to discover a meaning that is not of our own making. The "technical" worldview that follows from this vision is now so dominant that truth has come to be seen as coinciding with the possible. But when the sole criterion of truth is efficiency and utility, development is automatically denied. True development does not consist primarily in "doing". The key to development is a mind capable of thinking in technological terms and grasping the fully human meaning of human activities within the context of the holistic meaning of the individual's being. Even when we work through satellites or through remote electronic impulses, our actions always remain

---

[152] Cf. Paul VI, Apostolic Letter *Octogesima Adveniens*, 29: *loc. cit.*, 420.

human, an expression of our responsible freedom. Technology is highly attractive because it draws us out of our physical limitations and broadens our horizon. *But human freedom is authentic only when it responds to the fascination of technology with decisions that are the fruit of moral responsibility.* Hence the pressing need for formation in an ethically responsible use of technology. Moving beyond the fascination that technology exerts, we must reappropriate the true meaning of freedom, which is not an intoxication with total autonomy, but a response to the call of being, beginning with our own personal being.

71. This deviation from solid humanistic principles that a technical mindset can produce is seen today in certain technological applications in the fields of development and peace. Often the development of peoples is considered a matter of financial engineering, the freeing up of markets, the removal of tariffs, investment in production, and institutional reforms—in other words, a purely technical matter. All these factors are of great importance, but we have to ask why technical choices made thus far have yielded rather mixed results. We need to think hard about the cause. Development will never be fully guaranteed through

automatic or impersonal forces, whether they derive from the market or from international politics. *Development is impossible without upright men and women, without financiers and politicians whose consciences are finely attuned to the requirements of the common good.* Both professional competence and moral consistency are necessary. When technology is allowed to take over, the result is confusion between ends and means, such that the sole criterion for action in business is thought to be the maximization of profit, in politics the consolidation of power, and in science the findings of research. Often, underneath the intricacies of economic, financial, and political interconnections, there remain misunderstandings, hardships, and injustice. The flow of technological know-how increases, but it is those in possession of it who benefit, while the situation on the ground for the peoples who live in its shadow remains unchanged: for them there is little chance of emancipation.

72. Even peace can run the risk of being considered a technical product, merely the outcome of agreements between governments or of initiatives aimed at ensuring effective economic aid. It is true that *peace-building* requires the constant interplay of diplomatic contacts, economic, technological, and

cultural exchanges, agreements on common projects, as well as joint strategies to curb the threat of military conflict and to root out the underlying causes of terrorism. Nevertheless, if such efforts are to have lasting effects, they must be based on values rooted in the truth of human life. That is, the voice of the peoples affected must be heard, and their situation must be taken into consideration, if their expectations are to be correctly interpreted. One must align oneself, so to speak, with the unsung efforts of so many individuals deeply committed to bringing peoples together and to facilitating development on the basis of love and mutual understanding. Among them are members of the Christian faithful, involved in the great task of upholding the fully human dimension of development and peace.

73. Linked to technological development is the increasingly pervasive presence of the *means of social communications*. It is almost impossible today to imagine the life of the human family without them. For better or for worse, they are so integral a part of life today that it seems quite absurd to maintain that they are neutral—and hence unaffected by any moral considerations concerning people. Often such views, stressing the strictly technical nature of the media,

effectively support their subordination to economic interests intent on dominating the market and, not least, to attempts to impose cultural
models that serve ideological and political agen-
das. Given the media's fundamental importance in engineering changes in attitude towards
reality and the human person, we must reflect
carefully on their influence, especially in regard
to the ethical-cultural dimension of globalization and the development of peoples in solidarity. Mirroring what is required for an ethical
approach to globalization and development, so
too the *meaning and purpose of the media must be
sought within an anthropological perspective.* This
means that they can have a *civilizing effect* not
only when, thanks to technological development, they increase the possibilities of com-
municating information, but above all when
they are geared towards a vision of the person
and the common good that reflects truly universal values. Just because social communications increase the possibilities of interconnection
and the dissemination of ideas, it does not follow that they promote freedom or internation-
alize development and democracy for all. To
achieve goals of this kind, they need to focus
on promoting the dignity of persons and peoples; they need to be clearly inspired by charity and placed at the service of truth, of the

good, and of natural and supernatural fraternity. In fact, human freedom is intrinsically linked with these higher values. The media can make an important contribution towards the growth in communion of the human family and the *ethos* of society when they are used to promote universal participation in the common search for what is just.

74. A particularly crucial battleground in today's cultural struggle between the supremacy of technology and human moral responsibility is the field of *bioethics*, where the very possibility of integral human development is radically called into question. In this most delicate and critical area, the fundamental question asserts itself forcefully: is man the product of his own labors or does he depend on God? Scientific discoveries in this field and the possibilities of technological intervention seem so advanced as to force a choice between two types of reasoning: reason open to transcendence or reason closed within immanence. We are presented with a clear *either/or*. Yet the rationality of a self-centered use of technology proves to be irrational because it implies a decisive rejection of meaning and value. It is no coincidence that closing the door to transcendence brings one up short against a difficulty: how

could being emerge from nothing; how could intelligence be born from chance?[153] Faced with these dramatic questions, reason and faith can come to each other's assistance. Only together will they save man. *Entranced by an exclusive reliance on technology, reason without faith is doomed to flounder in an illusion of its own omnipotence. Faith without reason risks being cut off from everyday life.*[154]

75. Paul VI had already recognized and drawn attention to the global dimension of the social question.[155] Following his lead, we need to affirm today that *the social question has become a radically anthropological question,* in the sense that it concerns not just how life is conceived but also how it is manipulated, as biotechnology places it increasingly under man's control. *In vitro* fertilization, embryo research, the possibility of manufacturing clones and human hybrids: all this is now emerging and being promoted in today's highly disillusioned culture,

---

[153] Cf. Benedict XVI, *Address to the Participants in the Fourth National Congress of the Church in Italy,* Verona, 19 October 2006; *idem, Homily at Mass,* Islinger Feld, Regensburg, 12 September 2006.

[154] Cf. Congregation for the Doctrine of the Faith, Instruction on Certain Bioethical Questions *Dignitas Personae* (8 September 2008): *AAS* 100 (2008), 858–887.

[155] Cf. Encyclical Letter *Populorum Progressio,* 3: *loc. cit.,* 258.

which believes it has mastered every mystery because the origin of life is now within our grasp. Here we see the clearest expression of technology's supremacy. In this type of culture, the conscience is simply invited to take note of technological possibilities. Yet we must not underestimate the disturbing scenarios that threaten our future or the powerful new instruments that the "culture of death" has at its disposal. To the tragic and widespread scourge of abortion we may well have to add in the future—indeed, it is already surreptitiously present—the systematic eugenic programming of births. At the other end of the spectrum, a pro-euthanasia mindset is making inroads as an equally damaging assertion of control over life that under certain circumstances is deemed no longer worth living. Underlying these scenarios are cultural viewpoints that deny human dignity. These practices in turn foster a materialistic and mechanistic understanding of human life. Who could measure the negative effects of this kind of mentality for development? How can we be surprised by the indifference shown towards situations of human degradation when such indifference extends even to our attitude towards what is and is not human? What is astonishing is the arbitrary and selective determination of what to put forward today as worthy of respect. Insignificant matters are considered shocking, yet unprecedented injustices seem to be widely tolerated. While the poor of the world continue knocking on the doors of the rich, the world of affluence runs the risk of no longer hearing those knocks on account of a conscience that can no longer distinguish what is human. God reveals man to himself; reason and faith work hand in hand to demonstrate to us what is good, provided we want to see it; the natural law, in which creative Reason shines forth, reveals our greatness but also our wretchedness insofar as we fail to recognize the call to moral truth.

76. One aspect of the contemporary technological mindset is the tendency to consider the problems and emotions of the interior life from a purely psychological point of view, even to the point of neurological reductionism. In this way man's interiority is emptied of its meaning, and gradually our awareness of the human soul's ontological depths, as probed by the saints, is lost. *The question of development is closely bound up with our understanding of the human soul,* insofar as we often reduce the self to the psyche and confuse the soul's health with emotional well-being. These over-simplifications stem

from a profound failure to understand the spiritual life, and they obscure the fact that the development of individuals and peoples depends partly on the resolution of problems of a spiritual nature. *Development must include not just material growth but also spiritual growth,* since the human person is a "unity of body and soul",[156] born of God's creative love and destined for eternal life. The human being develops when he grows in the spirit, when his soul comes to know itself and the truths that God has implanted deep within, when he enters into dialogue with himself and his Creator. When he is far away from God, man is unsettled and ill at ease. Social and psychological alienation and the many neuroses that afflict affluent societies are attributable in part to spiritual factors. A prosperous society, highly developed in material terms but weighing heavily on the soul, is not of itself conducive to authentic development. The new forms of slavery to drugs and the lack of hope into which so many people fall can be explained not only in sociological and psychological terms but also in essentially spiritual terms. The emptiness in which the soul feels abandoned, despite the

---

[156] Second Vatican Ecumenical Council, Pastoral Constitution on the Church in the Modern World *Gaudium et Spes*, 14.

availability of countless therapies for body and psyche, leads to suffering. *There cannot be holistic development and universal common good unless people's spiritual and moral welfare is taken into account,* considered in their totality as body and soul.

77. The supremacy of technology tends to prevent people from recognizing anything that cannot be explained in terms of matter alone. Yet everyone experiences the many immaterial and spiritual dimensions of life. Knowing is not simply a material act, since the object that is known always conceals something beyond the empirical datum. All our knowledge, even the most simple, is always a minor miracle, since it can never be fully explained by the material instruments that we apply to it. In every truth there is something more than we would have expected; in the love that we receive there is always an element that surprises us. We should never cease to marvel at these things. In all knowledge and in every act of love the human soul experiences something "over and above", which seems very much like a gift that we receive or a height to which we are raised. The development of individuals and peoples is likewise located on a height, if we consider *the spiritual dimension*

that must be present if such development is to be authentic. It requires new eyes and a new heart, capable of *rising above a materialistic vision of human events*, capable of glimpsing in development the "beyond" that technology cannot give. By following this path, it is possible to pursue the integral human development that takes its direction from the driving force of charity in truth.

CONCLUSION

78. Without God man neither knows which way to go nor even understands who he is. In the face of the enormous problems surrounding the development of peoples, which almost make us yield to discouragement, we find solace in the sayings of our Lord Jesus Christ, who teaches us: "Apart from me you can do nothing" (*Jn* 15:5) and then encourages us: "I am with you always, to the close of the age" (*Mt* 28:20). As we contemplate the vast amount of work to be done, we are sustained by our faith that God is present alongside those who come together in his name to work for justice. Paul VI recalled in *Populorum Progressio* that man cannot bring about his own progress unaided, because by himself he cannot establish an authentic humanism. Only if we are aware of our calling, as individuals and as a community, to be part of God's family as his sons and daughters will we be able to generate a new vision and muster new energy in the service of a truly integral humanism. The greatest service to development, then, is a Christian humanism[157] that enkindles charity and

---

[157] Cf. Paul VI, Encyclical Letter *Populorum Progressio*, 42: *loc. cit.*, 278.

takes its lead from truth, accepting both as a lasting gift from God. Openness to God makes us open towards our brothers and sisters and towards an understanding of life as a joyful task to be accomplished in a spirit of solidarity. On the other hand, ideological rejection of God and an atheism of indifference, oblivious to the Creator and at risk of becoming equally oblivious to human values, constitute some of the chief obstacles to development today. *A humanism which excludes God is an inhuman humanism.* Only a humanism open to the Absolute can guide us in the promotion and building of forms of social and civic life—structures, institutions, culture, and *ethos*—without exposing us to the risk of becoming ensnared by the fashions of the moment. Awareness of God's undying love sustains us in our laborious and stimulating work for justice and the development of peoples, amid successes and failures, in the ceaseless pursuit of a just ordering of human affairs. *God's love calls us to move beyond the limited and the ephemeral, it gives us the courage to continue seeking and working for the benefit of all,* even if this cannot be achieved immediately and if what we are able to achieve, alongside political authorities and those working in the field of economics, is always less than we might wish.[158] God gives us the strength to fight and to suffer for love of the common good, because he is our All, our greatest hope.

79. *Development needs Christians with their arms raised towards God* in prayer, Christians moved by the knowledge that truth-filled love, *caritas in veritate*, from which authentic development proceeds, is not produced by us, but given to us. For this reason, even in the most difficult and complex times, besides recognizing what is happening, we must above all else turn to God's love. Development requires attention to the spiritual life, a serious consideration of the experiences of trust in God, spiritual fellowship in Christ, reliance upon God's providence and mercy, love and forgiveness, self-denial, acceptance of others, justice, and peace. All this is essential if "hearts of stone" are to be transformed into "hearts of flesh" (*Ezek* 36:26), rendering life on earth "divine" and thus more worthy of humanity. All this is *of man*, because man is the subject of his own existence; and at the same time it is *of God*, because God is at the beginning and end of all that

---

[158] Cf. Benedict XVI, Encyclical Letter *Spe Salvi*, 35: *loc. cit.*, 1013–1014.

is good, all that leads to salvation: "the world
or life or death or the present or the future,
all are yours; and you are Christ's; and Christ
is God's" (*1 Cor* 3:22–23). Christians long
for the entire human family to call upon
God as "Our Father!" In union with the only-
begotten Son, may all people learn to pray to
the Father and to ask him, in the words
that Jesus himself taught us, for the grace to
glorify him by living according to his will,
to receive the daily bread that we need, to
be understanding and generous towards our
debtors, not to be tempted beyond our limits, and to be delivered from evil (cf. *Mt*
6:9–13).

At the conclusion of the *Pauline Year*, I gladly
express this hope in the Apostle's own words,
taken from the *Letter to the Romans*: "Let love
be genuine; hate what is evil, hold fast to
what is good; love one another with broth-
erly affection; outdo one another in showing
honor" (*Rom* 12:9–10). May the Virgin
Mary—proclaimed *Mater Ecclesiae* by Paul VI
and honored by Christians as *Speculum Iusti-
tiae* and *Regina Pacis*—protect us and obtain
for us, through her heavenly intercession, the
strength, hope, and joy necessary to continue
to dedicate ourselves with generosity to the

task of bringing about the "*development of the whole man and of all men*".[159]

Given in Rome, at Saint Peter's, on 29 June, the Solemnity of the Holy Apostles Peter and Paul, in the year 2009, the fifth of my Pontificate.

---

[159] Paul VI, Encyclical Letter *Populorum Progressio*, 42: *loc. cit.*, 278.